The American Civil War

THE EMERGENCE OF TOTAL WARFARE

Robert A. Doughty
United States Military Academy

Roy K. Flint
United States Military Academy

George C. Herring
University of Kentucky

John A. Lynn
University of Illinois

Ira D. Gruber
Rice University

Mark Grimsley
The Ohio State University

Donald D. Horward
Florida State University

Williamson Murray
The Ohio State University

D. C. Heath and Company
Lexington, Massachusetts   Toronto

Address editorial correspondence to:

D. C. Heath and Company
125 Spring Street
Lexington, MA 02173

Acquisitions: *James Miller*
Development: *Pat Wakeley*
Editorial Production: *Melissa Ray*
Design: *Alwyn R. Velásquez*
Photo Research: *Picture Research Consultants, Inc./Sandi Rygiel & Pembroke Herbert*
Art Editing: *Diane Grossman*
Production Coordination: *Richard Tonachel*

The views expressed herein are those of the authors and do not purport to reflect the position of the United States Military Academy, the Department of the Army, or the Department of Defense.

10 9 8 7 6 5 4 3 2 1

PREFACE

The *American Civil War* was first published as a part of a larger history, *Warfare in the Western World*. We wrote that larger history to provide a coherent, readable, and authoritative account of the past four centuries of military operations in the West—to explain, as clearly as possible, how the waging of war has changed from one era to another since the beginning of the seventeenth century. Although we examined the underlying developments in population, agriculture, industry, technology, and politics that affected warfare, we focused on the employment of armed forces. We were most interested in operations, in the conduct of relatively large forces across a specific theater of war. In short, we set out to write a sound and readable history of military operations in the West since 1600, a history that would appeal to students, general readers, and anyone seeking an authoritative reference on warfare.

Like its parent volumes, *The American Civil War* was designed to provide a coherent, readable, and authoritative history of military operations—in this instance, of operations during one of the central events in the history of the United States and of Western warfare. It is now published separately because its author, Mark Grimsley, has succeeded especially well in what he intended to do and because the American Civil War remains a fascinating subject. Grimsley reminds us how important the Civil War was in United States history—in the preservation of the Union, the abolition of slavery, the definition of American civil rights, and the commitment to ideals that have given the nation its peculiar vitality. He also makes clear how important the Civil War was in the larger history of warfare—in the prolonged but steady increase in the comprehensiveness and destructiveness of military operations.

Indeed, the Civil War was one of the most significant events in the emergence of total warfare in the Western world. In the wars of the French Revolution and Napoleon, Europeans embarked on wars of survival and conquest. They employed conscription, ideology, and simplified tactics to create armies of unprecedented size and power; and they used those armies to engage and destroy enemy forces in campaigns of exceptional scale, speed, and decisiveness. Napoleon even managed to rouse spontaneous and fanatical popular resistance in Spain and Russia. But in the American Civil War, the people of the United States went beyond Europeans in waging total war as an instrument of national policy. Northern commanders hoped at first to fight a relatively short and bloodless war that would restore the Union without alienating the people of the South. They tried to win by blockading Southern ports and capturing the capital of the Confederacy—a strategy that soon failed. Rifled weapons gave the armies on the defensive clear advantages, and Northern commanders could not easily destroy the armies of the South or capture fortified positions. Frustrated, Northerners gradually began to wage total war against the South. They sought not only to wear away Confederate forces in campaigns of attrition but also to exhaust the South by freeing slaves, obliterating farms and factories, and breaking the will of the people. In making war against all the resources of the Confederacy, the United States eventually won the war, preserved the Union, and came closer than any other nineteenth-century state to the total warfare of the twentieth century.

Grimsley's success in locating the American Civil War in the broader history of the United States and of warfare in the Western world is a tribute to his knowledge of the subject and his talent for synthesis. It is also a tribute to the work of scores of other scholars. He, like the other authors of *Warfare in the Western World*, has benefitted from the writings and comments of many specialists and colleagues. We are all particularly indebted to Richard Kohn and John Shy, who read carefully an entire draft of the text and drew on their remarkable understanding of military history and sharp critical judgment to suggest ways of improving the whole. We are grateful to all who have had a part in creating *Warfare in the Western World* in general and *The American Civil War* in particular. We do not imagine that we will have satisfied our critics; we do hope that they and other readers will continue to share their knowledge of warfare with us.

R. A. D. and I. D. G.

CONTENTS IN BRIEF

CONTENTS

MAP SYMBOLS

The symbols shown below are used on the maps in this volume. Most of the symbols suggest the organization of units in particular campaigns or battles. The reader should understand that the organization of military units has changed over time and has varied from army to army or even within armies. For example, the composition and size of Napoleon's corps varied within his own army and differed from those of his opponents; they also differed dramatically from those of armies later in the nineteenth century. The symbols thus indicate the organization of a unit at a particular time and do not indicate its precise composition or size.

Division

Corps

Army

Army Group

Cavalry Screen

Armor

Airborne

Fort

Mine

Bridge

Boundary between Units

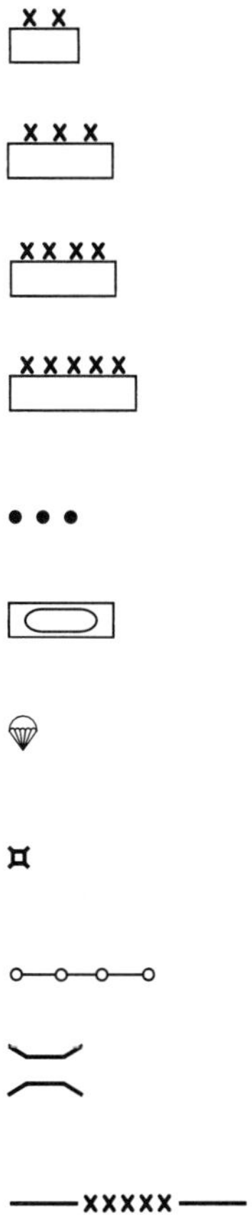

LIST OF MAPS

1

AMERICAN MILITARY POLICY, 1783–1860: THE BEGINNINGS OF PROFESSIONALISM

Arming the New Nation, 1783–1846

The Mexican War

Technological Adaptation and Strategic Thought

Considering that it was a nation founded in blood, the United States took a notably relaxed attitude toward its military defense during the years between 1783 and 1860. Americans created only a very modest standing army and navy, resented efforts to professionalize the officer corps, and for a long time regarded the permanent armed forces as inimical to sound republican principles. Scornful and suspicious of regular armed forces, they preferred to regard the militia as the chief reliance for defense. Yet in practice, Americans neglected the militia system even more than they did the despised standing army, so that by the mid-nineteenth century the system was practically moribund.

Indeed, in nearly every respect, during its first seventy-five years the United States possessed an uneven military policy and a ramshackle military establishment. Yet during the same period it managed to drive the Native Americans beyond the Mississippi River, hold its own in a second full-scale war with the British, and conquer vast new territories in an amoral but highly successful conflict with Mexico. Judged by results, the new republic turned in a creditable military performance.

Although partly due to circumstance or good fortune, some of America's martial success stemmed from the early emergence of a professional officer corps. Sobered by a brush with disaster during the War of 1812, the army overhauled its bureaucracy, inaugurated an orderly system of officer recruitment, and established professional standards of conduct, particularly through the reform of the U.S. Military Academy. Meanwhile

1

Congress, despite continuing lip service to the militia, adopted a cadre system that tacitly made the regular army the centerpiece of the nation's land-defense system. Within the new environment, officers increasingly viewed their work as a lifelong calling. Careers grew longer, a distinctive corporate identity emerged, and officers rapidly divorced themselves from partisan politics. By the time of the Civil War, the army officer corps had established an identity, ethos, and outlook that greatly assisted the full flowering of military professionalism in the late nineteenth and early twentieth centuries.

Arming the New Nation, 1783–1846

In its earliest stages, the permanent American military establishment was the product of two factors. First, the political faction known as the Federalists believed the new central government had to develop a significant *national* army and navy. Second, a prolonged period of international upheaval underscored the need for adequate armed forces. Even so, the creation of a permanent military establishment did not occur without significant opposition. Many Americans were unhappy with the idea of creating a standing army. But a significant minority, especially those who had served in the Continental Army, agreed with George Washington, who understood the fear of a standing army but also believed that fear should not be blindly heeded. Unlike European mercenaries who had no stake in the political order, Washington argued, an American army was composed of citizens with common interests—"one people embarked on one cause; acting on the same principle and the same end." Since those interests were the same as that of the larger community, the army logically posed no threat to liberty. Eventually Washington's view triumphed, but it took thirty years, a number of small military incidents, and a major war before that occurred.

The Creation of Permanent Military Forces

After the war with Great Britain ended in 1783, the Confederation turned to the matter of a permanent peacetime military establishment that would be able to police the land and maritime frontier, defend against a full-scale invasion, and help maintain internal order. In 1783 a Congressional committee chaired by Alexander Hamilton asked Washington for his opinion concerning the requirements of such an establishment. Washington responded with "Sentiments on a Peace Establishment," a four-point program that became the basis of the nationalist agenda. First, a small regular army (2,631 officers and men) was required to "overawe" Indians and guard against incursions from Canada and Spanish Florida. Second, a "respectable and well-established Militia" was also needed, preferably under federal as well as state control, with the central government imposing uniformity in training, arms, and organization. It should have two tiers: a volunteer militia to be kept in an advanced state of readiness, and a common militia composed of the remaining male population of military age. Third, the national government must establish arsenals and factories to support the armed forces. And fourth, it must create military academies to foster military science.

The Hamilton Committee greeted Washington's proposals with enthusiasm and modeled its own report along similar lines. But Congress, then predominantly antinationalist in tone, rejected the report. Rather than create a standing army, it elected to disband the Continental Army except for eighty men and a few officers to guard military stores. Instead it created the First American Regiment, composed of 700 militiamen (drawn from four states) to serve one year. This ad hoc arrangement—like the Confederation itself—proved inadequate, and when the Americans scrapped the Articles of Confederation in favor of a new Constitution, they attempted to create a more effective military establishment that would not jeopardize American liberties.

The solution was to divide control of the military establishment. The president would serve as commander-in-chief, but Congress would appropriate money for the armed forces, devise regulations for their government, and hold the authority to declare war. Control of the military establishment was further divided between the national government, which could create a national army and navy, and the states, which maintained control over the militia. A modest system of arsenals and munitions factories also sprang up, and in 1802 Congress authorized creation of a military academy at West Point, New York. (Naval officers continued to be trained aboard warships; Congress would not create the naval academy at Annapolis, Maryland, until 1845.)

Thus by the early years of the nineteenth century the United States possessed a land force roughly corresponding to the model outlined in "Sentiments on a Peace Establishment." The chief departure was the very limited federal control over the militia. Attempts to increase control—for example, to create the sort of volunteer or "federal select" militia favored by Washington—routinely failed. As a result, although in times of emergency the national government could mobilize the militia for a period of ninety days, it had little influence over the peacetime organization, regulation, training and equipment of the militia. Since most state governments were notoriously lax in such matters, the militia—supposedly the nation's chief reliance in wartime—was an uncertain patchwork of units without uniform organization, training, or equipment.

Old World Frictions

These developments occurred against a background of European revolution and war. Less than a year after the American Constitution went into operation, violent political upheaval erupted in France. With their own revolution just recently behind them, Americans watched the unfolding drama in France with more than passing interest. Indeed, as the months rolled on, the

French Revolution exerted an almost tidal pull on American political life. Then, in 1792, the new French republic declared war on Austria, inaugurating twenty-three years of near-continuous war that embroiled not only most of Europe but eventually the United States as well. Moreover, the unfolding French Revolution, as Americans alternately cheered its triumphs and deplored its excesses, deeply influenced the ongoing debate between two emerging factions in American politics: the Federalists, led by Alexander Hamilton, and their Republican opponents, led by Thomas Jefferson.

The Federalists were nationalist in their orientation, comfortable with an active central government, and wary of placing too much power in the hands of the common man. Although at first elated by the events in France, they soon grew to distrust the direction in which the French Revolution was moving. It seemed to have degenerated into radicalism and mob rule. In the burgeoning wars of the French Revolution, therefore, the Federalists usually supported the British, who were fighting against the French. The Republicans, however—more democratic and also suspicious of what seemed the "monarchist" tendencies of the Federalists—were not disillusioned by the excesses of the French Revolution and continued to prefer the French. Officially, the United States was neutral.

The question of whether to back one side or the other had more than academic significance. The wars of the French Revolution were characterized not only by major land battles but also by a long campaign of economic warfare at sea. The British navy blockaded French ports; the French responded by sending out large numbers of privateers and commerce raiders to prowl the world's oceans. Since American merchants traded with both Britain and France, each side freely attacked American vessels bound for enemy ports.

Trouble began first with Great Britain, which routinely seized neutral ships carrying contraband goods to France. The Royal Navy captured 250 American merchant vessels before the Washington administration negotiated a treaty, ratified in 1795, in which the United States essentially accepted the British position on contraband in exchange for a promise that British troops would abandon a number of posts still illegally occupied on American soil. The French, however, interpreted the treaty as an American attempt to aid the British and eventually began seizing American merchant ships on the high seas. In 1798 a two-year undeclared naval war broke out between the United States and France.

These difficulties with Britain and France led to the early growth of the United States Navy. Begun in 1794 with the authorization of six frigates, the new navy at the height of the "Quasi-War" with France boasted fifty-four warships supported by more than a thousand armed merchant vessels. At about the same time Congress created a separate Department of the Navy and authorized construction of the first American ships of the line. American warships not only performed well against the French but also conducted a number of minor but dramatic punitive expeditions against several pirate states in North Africa.

By 1800, however, the Quasi-War had ended. Its main significance was to reinforce the need for adequate American armed forces, so that when the Republican party took power in 1801 with the accession of Thomas Jefferson as president, the Jeffersonians did not dismantle the military establishment created by the Federalists. To be sure, for a time they did reduce the size of the army and navy, mostly in response to a temporary reduction in European tensions. But they basically accepted and, in time, even enhanced the military institutions whose custodianship they inherited. And as a fresh cycle of wars began in 1805, the Jefferson administration found itself sliding into a new and grave crisis with Great Britain.

The War of 1812

Once again the British and French were locked in mortal combat (this time with Napoleon leading France), and once again the navies of both powers seized American and other neutral ships in a bid to throttle each other's commerce. Americans were furious with both nations, but of the two, Britain had the larger navy and thus the greater effect on American shipping. Jefferson and his successor, James Madison, made several efforts to force the British and French to respect American maritime rights, most notably an 1807 Embargo Act that essentially prohibited American exports. Based on the premise that the European powers needed the American trade and could not long do without it, the embargo was intended as an instrument of

Presidents Thomas Jefferson and James Madison tried to use economic coercion to force the British and French to respect U.S. maritime rights, but many Americans resented their policies, as suggested in this contemporary political cartoon. "Ograbme" is "Embargo" spelled backward.

economic coercion. In the short run, however, it hurt American merchants far more than Europeans and generated violent political opposition.

Forced to retreat from outright embargo, the Madison administration struggled to convince Congress to maintain some sort of economic coercion. But increasingly some members of the Republican party demanded that the administration should go farther and declare war on Great Britain. The seizure of American vessels seemed provocation enough, but on top of that the Royal Navy had for years forcibly impressed sailors—some of them U.S. citizens—from American-owned vessels. Further, many Americans living in the South and along the western frontier sought war for other reasons. Many westerners believed the British had been inciting Native American uprisings; they also thought that if war came, it might be possible to grab Canada. Similarly, southerners tended to suspect the British of plotting to seize New Orleans; they also noted that if war broke out they might be able to seize Florida from Spain, whose royal family was then allied with the British.

Madison himself was far from eager for war. But he grew convinced that economic coercion alone would never succeed, because the policy was based on a faulty premise. In earlier years, Britain might have depended on the United States for naval stores crucial to its fleet and seaborne empire. But the growing economic development of Canada gave Britain a viable alternative source and thereby gravely reduced the American bargaining posture. Only a credible threat against Canada could compel the British to respect American maritime rights.

Madison therefore reluctantly asked Congress for a declaration of war. He got one on June 18, 1812, but the margin of the vote was the narrowest for a declaration of war in U.S. history. To a man, the Federalist party rejected the necessity for military action. Deep political divisions persisted throughout the conflict itself, for few on either side tried to create bipartisan support for a struggle against a common foe.

The United States was woefully unprepared in 1812 to take on a major power like Great Britain. Despite recent legislation that authorized an increase to 35,000 men, when war broke out the regular army numbered just 7,000, scattered in various garrisons. A sustained war effort would thus have to be built upon volunteer militia companies backed by the common militia. The naval establishment was no better: just sixteen ships, seven of them frigates, plus swarms of small gunboats. Administrative support had improved little since 1775. Not only was the War Department inadequate to manage a substantial military effort, the federal government had limited ability to finance the war.

Given Canada's importance in Madison's calculations, an invasion of the province was the obvious American strategy. The province was only lightly defended and in theory the Americans should have been able to advance northward in overwhelming strength. Reality proved different. A prompt invasion necessarily depended upon the use of militia forces, yet these were under state control. The best invasion route was north along the Lake Champlain corridor toward Montreal, but the springboard for such an advance—New England—had the least enthusiasm for war of any region in the country.

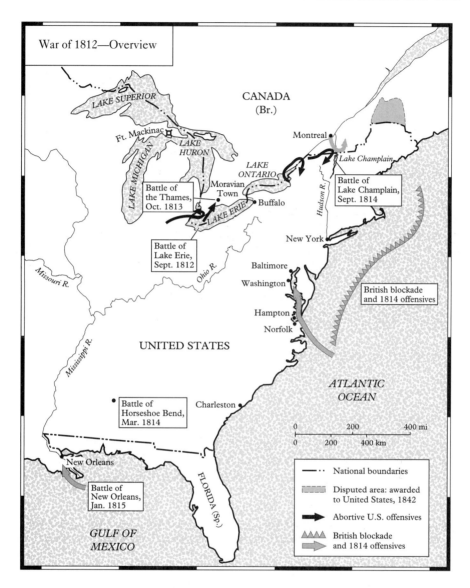

War of 1812—Overview

LAKE SUPERIOR

CANADA
(Br.)

Ft. Mackinac

LAKE
HURON

LAKE MICHIGAN

Montreal

Lake Champlain

LAKE
ONTARIO

Moravian
Town

Battle of
the Thames,
Oct. 1813

Buffalo

LAKE ERIE

Battle of
Lake Champlain,
Sept. 1814

Hudson R.

Battle of
Lake Erie,
Sept. 1812

Ohio R.

New York

Missouri R.

Baltimore

Washington

British blockade
and 1814 offensives

Hampton

Norfolk

UNITED STATES

Mississippi R.

ATLANTIC
OCEAN

Battle of
Horseshoe Bend,
Mar. 1814

Charleston

0   200   400 mi
0   200   400 km

New Orleans

FLORIDA (Sp.)

Battle of
New Orleans,
Jan. 1815

GULF OF
MEXICO

— · ·   National boundaries

Disputed area: awarded
to United States, 1842

Abortive U.S. offensives

British blockade
and 1814 offensives

Asked by Madison to mobilize their militias, the Federalist New England governors flatly refused, objecting that such forces were intended solely for local defense. A volatile political situation in New York further complicated efforts to mount an offensive into Canada. Instead of a rapid, victorious advance, therefore, practically nothing happened in the key Montreal sector.

By contrast, Americans living in the western frontier region were far more eager for war. There the problem was not so much to raise the necessary volunteers and militia as it was to equip, feed, and manage them. But the modest American government could do none of these things effectively. The initial American thrusts were poorly coordinated, understrength—and disastrous. Numerically inferior but better organized British troops repelled them, seized Detroit, and threatened Michigan Territory and Ohio.

In October 1813, Americans under Major General William Henry Harrison defeated a combined force of British and Indians in the Battle of the Thames, fought on the Lake Erie frontier. Coupled with Andrew Jackson's 1814 win at Horseshoe Bend, Harrison's victory broke the back of Native American resistance east of the Mississippi River.

Fortunately for the United States, Britain was too preoccupied with European matters to mount a major effort in North America. Thus in 1813 the United States had a chance to accomplish what it had failed to do in 1812. But again, poor leadership, inadequate administrative support, and disjointed efforts resulted in scant success. This was particularly true on the Niagara front, where a mixed bag of tactical successes and setbacks resulted in stalemate. Somewhat better results were achieved in the western Lake Erie region. Detroit was recaptured, and Commodore Oliver Hazard Perry destroyed a British squadron near Put-In Bay, Ohio. Major General William Henry Harrison entered Canada, won the Battle of the Thames against a combined British and Native American force, and slew Tecumseh, the great Shawnee chieftain. Yet while these successes secured the western U.S. frontier, they contributed little toward ending the war.

At sea the Royal Navy far outnumbered the diminutive U.S. Navy—even though the British had to concentrate on Napoleon until 1814. Consequently the British were able to blockade the American coast at will. Interestingly, for a long time they chose *not* to blockade New England, since they knew New Englanders generally opposed the war. Indeed the U.S. government even allowed a certain amount of trade with the enemy. American vessels sailed to Spain, for example, and supplied grain to Wellington's army. Even so, by 1814 the blockade had reduced merchant trade to 11 percent of prewar levels.

The blockade was loose enough, however, that U.S. warships had little difficulty getting to sea, and although they could scarcely compete for control of the ocean, American vessels performed very well at commerce-raiding and single-ship duels; sloops and 500 privateers seized over 1,300 British merchantmen. Nevertheless, the British still managed to supply forces in Canada and conduct raids against American coasts. These raids, small at first, expanded dramatically in 1814.

A common nineteenth-century saw declared that "God takes care of fools, drunkards, and the United States." In 1814, America needed providential help. After the defeat of Napoleon in the Saxon campaign of 1813, the British for the first time were able to send large forces across the Atlantic. About 40,000 arrived by year's end. These occupied much of Maine and expanded their raids along the coast. Fortunately for the United States, competent leaders had begun to emerge by this time, especially Jacob Brown, Edmund Gaines, Winfield Scott, and Andrew Jackson.

The United States began the year with two new offensives against Canada—one on the Niagara front and one along the Lake Champlain corridor. Neither came to much, but the Americans handled the Niagara operations much better tactically than the one along Lake Champlain. The British launched three offensives of their own: first, south from Canada via Lake Champlain, a thrust blunted in a naval battle on the lake in September; second, along the Chesapeake Bay, which resulted in the capture and burning of Washington but which failed to seize the privateering base of Baltimore, Maryland; and finally, up the Mississippi River against New Orleans. Forces under Andrew Jackson, in the largest battle of the war, decisively halted this last attack on January 15, 1815. But by then the war was officially over. Six weeks earlier the United States and Great Britain had signed the Treaty of Ghent.

Why did the British, who clearly held the advantage, choose to end the war? For one thing, they could not identify a plausible way to win it. After the Lake Champlain offensive was rebuffed, the Duke of Wellington commented that the United States had no vulnerable center of gravity. "I do not know where you could carry on . . . an operation which would be so injurious to the Americans as to force them to sue for peace." Moreover, with the defeat of Napoleon the reasons for war had largely disappeared. Thus, both sides willingly accepted a peace nominally based on the status quo antebellum.

In some respects the United States achieved significant benefits from the conflict. The war had furnished an opportunity to thrash yet again Native Americans, who were the main losers in the contest. Tecumseh's death at the Battle of the Thames forever ended the most significant threat to white America's settlement of the Old Northwest, while in Alabama, at the 1814 Battle of Horseshoe Bend, Andrew Jackson defeated the Creeks and forced them to cede 23 million acres of land.

But for the most part, the poor American showing in the War of 1812 underscored the essential weakness of its military system. Unreflective nationalists might crow over victories like the battles of Lake Erie and New Orleans, but more reflective observers realized that the country had narrowly

The Battle of New Orleans. This idealized postwar engraving captures the War of 1812 as Americans liked to remember it, with homespun heroes fending off the best Great Britain could send against them. But such triumphs were few, and after the war American policy makers made several needed military reforms.

escaped disaster. The militia had proven unequal to its key role in American defense. The regular army had done better but still suffered from leadership problems, particularly in the war's early stages. The serious administrative deficiencies demonstrated that the War Department required substantial reform, and in the years that followed, American policy makers took significant steps to improve the situation.

Early Attempts to Professionalize

After 1815 the United States entered what one historian has called an "era of free security" in which the country faced little external threat to its existence. He meant that the United States did not need seriously to concern itself with threats from abroad and thus did not have to maintain a sizable army and navy. With minimal risk of foreign invasion, the American armed forces functioned mostly as a "frontier constabulary," a kind of national police force to assist western settlement, intervene in disputes between whites and Native Americans, enforce federal authority, and protect maritime commerce.

Strategically, however, the chief mission of the American army and navy was to defend against foreign invasions. Americans, while continuing to reject creation of a large navy that could challenge an enemy fleet for command of the sea, did permit a modest increase in the number of warships. The navy, then, would function as the first line of defense. The second line was an extensive network of coastal defenses that would hamper an invasion.

Work on such a fortification system began before the War of 1812 but really took off afterward. It consisted of a series of casemate forts guarding not only major harbors but also most navigable inlets. Fifty sites were identified at first; the number eventually ran much higher. The coastal forts were not intended as an absolute defense against attack but rather to ward off sudden raids and force an attacker to come ashore in areas distant from important military objectives. That, in turn, would allow sufficient time to mobilize the militia, which would slow the progress of any invader while a large citizen-based force could be built around the regular army.

Policy makers disagreed about how much reliance to place on the militia, however. Some continued to believe it could function effectively in wartime; others, more skeptical, thought the regular army would have to play the principal role even in a conflict's early stages. The key proponent of the second view was John C. Calhoun, a former "War Hawk" congressman from South Carolina, who became secretary of war in October 1817. Obliged by Congress to reduce the size of the army after the war, he sought to do so without destroying its ability to respond quickly in the event of a crisis. To this end he proposed a cadre system (often called an "expansible army" system) whereby a relatively small peacetime army could be rapidly built up in time of war. He proposed an army that would contain just 6,316 men but would have an officer corps and organization sufficient for an army of 11,558 men. Peacetime units would be kept at about 50 percent strength. In wartime the army could be nearly doubled just by filling out units to wartime strength using federal volunteers; and by adding 288 officers, the army could absorb enough additional privates and noncommissioned officers to raise the total to 19,035 officers and men.

The effect of this cadre proposal was subtle but profound. On the one hand, Congress declined to adopt the plan in its original form—it was too advanced for the time. Republicans had become more comfortable with the army's political reliability, but not enough to acknowledge the regular army unambiguously as the nation's main line of defense. Yet the plan eventually adopted was, in fact, a modified version of the cadre system that tacitly acknowledged Calhoun's central point: that in the event of war, the regular army was the most reliable means of national defense. From that point onward, the regular army officer corps suffered none of the wide-ranging shifts in size that characterized its early years. The frequent deep reductions in force had led many young officers to regard military service as a temporary vocation only. Within the more stable environment created by the Calhoun reforms, young officers could now consider military service a viable, lifelong career. As a result they remained officers longer, took their duties more seriously, and became more competent than their pre–War of 1812 counterparts.

Yet another important postwar development was a major revival at the U.S. Military Academy that marked the real beginning of its traditions. The catalyst was Captain Sylvanus Thayer, appointed West Point superintendent in 1817. Thayer established a four-year curriculum, inaugurated a system that ranked cadets according to merit, and introduced the emphasis on engineering and mathematics that would characterize West Point for several decades. Other indications of a budding professionalism included a more efficient military bureau system and two military schools of practice—one for artillery at Fort Monroe, one for infantry at Leavenworth, Kansas—which flourished briefly until fiscal constraints led to their closure in the late 1830s. Finally, a number of officers began to publish in journals devoted to the study of their craft.

Even so, it would be wrong to mistake these developments for the emergence of a fully mature, professionalized army. True professionalism still lay over a half-century in the future. The Indian pacification duties of this period formed a powerful distraction to the U.S. Army's preparations to wage European-style warfare. A second distraction was the nation's insistence that both the army and navy assist the protean economic expansion that dominated the years after the War of 1812. On land, army engineers deepened harbors and surveyed the routes for turnpikes and—a bit later—railroads as well. At sea, naval officers undertook voyages of exploration, mapped the coastline, and created hydrological charts as aids to navigation. Such duties not only diverted officers from the study of warfare but also shaped their ideas concerning what the military profession was all about. For some, overawing the Indians and surveying the wilderness seemed to have become their primary purpose in life.

Further hampering the professionalizing impetus were two powerful contrary forces: continued suspicions of the regular military establishment and a continuing belief that any man of good character was capable of exercising military leadership. Logically, both developments should have meant a continued commitment to a strong militia. But by the 1830s an odd situation had developed. On the one hand, politicians and citizens still praised the

This whimsical, faintly mocking view of a pre–Civil War militia muster reflects the decline of a venerable American military institution. Though the minuteman tradition remained strong in rhetoric, the actual militia began a steep decline after the War of 1812 and by the time of the Civil War was practically moribund.

militia as a bulwark of liberty. On the other, everyone had long since realized that the militia was, in practice, more or less a joke. Musters became less frequent, militiamen received little or no serious training, and their weapons and equipment were antiquated and poorly maintained.

The federal government could not, and the states would not, reform the militia. Indeed, some states abolished compulsory militia service altogether. Fortunately, volunteer companies took up some of the slack and maintained the tradition of the citizen-soldier. These were units that originally existed independently of the statewide militia systems, although many were later incorporated into them. Often they were the only functional part of the militia. Initially most were run as elite social societies. One had to have a modicum of wealth to join since volunteers bought their own uniforms and drill instructors cost money. Members carefully screened new recruits for good moral fiber and gentlemanly qualities. Over time, clerks, artisans, and laborers formed their own volunteer companies. So did immigrant groups, especially the Irish and Germans. After 1840 some states made the volunteer companies their entire "active militia" force.

The military value of these volunteer units was problematic. Although they provided their own uniforms, they often borrowed their weapons from state armories and rented their horses. They were also usually too small to be of great military significance—many contained about forty to fifty men. And they tended to emphasize martial dash and enthusiasm rather than serious tactical training. Still they provided a substantial reservoir of military experience. A number of future Civil War generals, including some very good ones, served in volunteer units.

Thus, by the mid-1840s, the United States had acquired a basic land-force policy characterized by de facto reliance on a small, peacetime regular army, coupled with the realization that the standing forces would have to be supplemented by a substantial contingent of citizen-soldiers. The available pool of citizen-soldiers varied widely in terms of organization, training, and equipment, but the general standard was low. Americans seldom worried about this, however. The absence of a serious foreign threat and a continued belief in the inherent military prowess of patriotic American males further sustained their confidence.

The Mexican War

Expansion was the hallmark of U.S. foreign policy during this period. Many Americans agreed with the newspaperman John L. O'Sullivan when he declaimed that their nation had a "manifest destiny" to possess all of North America. Examples of this conviction were legion. Already the United States had made two unsuccessful grabs for Canada; had acquired the Louisiana territory from France and Florida from Spain; and had briefly courted armed conflict with Great Britain before agreeing to divide the Oregon Country at the 49th Parallel. Then in 1845 Congress annexed Texas,

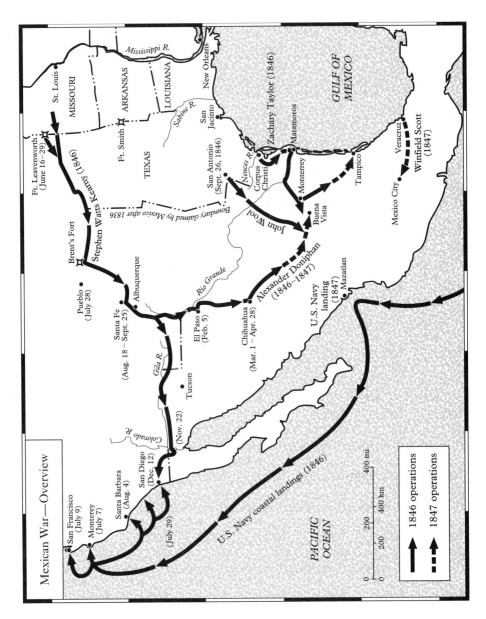

Mexican War—Overview

which Mexico still considered a wayward province in revolt, and thereby took a long step toward a major war. The first clashes occurred between U.S. and Mexican forces in 1846; sixteen months later the United States won a resounding triumph and added vast new territories to its already sprawling domain.

Origins and Objectives

Until 1836, Texas had been a province of Mexico. The Mexican government had welcomed American settlement in Texas, only to see a torrent of

Americans flood the province, swamp the ethnic Mexican population, and eventually rise up in an open bid for complete independence. This Texas Revolution culminated in triumph when, after initial setbacks at the Alamo and Goliad, the Texans defeated a Mexican army at the Battle of San Jacinto on April 21, 1836. After ten years as a separate republic, Texas joined the Union in July 1845. Relations between the United States and Mexico rapidly deteriorated, for Mexico had never relinquished its claim to the region.

American ambitions did not end with Texas. A number of Americans were also interested in Upper California and New Mexico, two northern provinces only tenuously under Mexican control. American merchants and politicians especially coveted the magnificent San Francisco harbor, widely regarded as the key to Far Eastern trade. President James K. Polk shared this expansionist vision, and while it is probably not true that he deliberately engineered a military confrontation with Mexico, indisputably he wanted California and New Mexico and was not particular about how he got them. His aggressive policies openly courted war.

Tensions between the United States and Mexico increased when Polk sent an American army into Texas led by Major General Zachary Taylor. After training seven months at Corpus Christi, Taylor's army crossed the Nueces River, the border between Texas and Mexico as the Mexicans understood it, and advanced to the Rio Grande, the border insisted upon by the Texans. For two weeks, Mexican and American forces glared at one another across the disputed boundary. The situation grew more intense, and in April 1846 the Mexicans attacked an American scouting party. "Hostilities," Taylor tersely informed Washington, "may now be considered as commenced."

Like the struggle of 1812–1814, the war was a highly partisan affair for Americans. This time the prowar camp was the Democratic party. Most members of the rival Whig party opposed it on principle, arguing (correctly)

General Zachary Taylor's Mexican War exploits helped make him president, but "Old Rough and Ready," as his soldiers called him, was in many respects a throwback to the amateurism of the War of 1812.

that the United States had no valid claims south of the Nueces. Antislavery Democrats and Whigs also charged that the war's purpose was to spread slavery and thus increase the political power of the southern states. Yet Whig opposition was less united and intransigent than the Federalists had been during the War of 1812. Although Mexico had clearly been provoked, most Whigs believed they could not refuse to support American troops now that they were engaged in combat.

Even so, real enthusiasm for the war tended to be confined politically to the Democratic party and geographically to the South. Because of the conflict's sectional and party overtones, manpower policy was essentially a political question with military implications. Given the soft support for the war, especially in the northeast, the Polk administration decided, by and large, not to use militia. Instead the regular army would double its existing units to 15,000 by filling them up to full strength. Congress also authorized the raising of 50,000 volunteers, most of whom were summoned by Polk from southern states, where support for the war was strongest.

American prewar planning was much better than it had been before the War of 1812. The United States had positioned troops to seize Mexican territory quickly. In addition to Taylor's army along the Texas border, American agents and an "exploring party" under John C. Frémont were in California; there were also naval units off the California shore. Another force under Colonel Stephen Kearny marched against Santa Fe two days after war was declared in May 1846.

American strategists essentially faced two problems. The first was to project U.S. strength into the lands they wanted; this occurred promptly after the declaration of war. The second was to get Mexico to accept an imposed settlement; this proved much trickier. Initially the Polk administration thought it could compel Mexico to the negotiating table by securing California and New Mexico and then holding a few of Mexico's northern provinces as bargaining chips. When that did not work, the Americans finally mounted a remarkable expedition to seize Mexico City itself.

Taylor in Northern Mexico

The Polk administration had entrusted about 4,000 men—most of the regular army—to General Taylor. Dubbed "Old Rough and Ready" by his men, Taylor dressed casually and spoke bluntly. He had as little use for rarefied notions of strategy and tactics as he did for the regulation uniform. In many respects he was a throwback to the amateurish generalship of the War of 1812, but he inspired his troops with confidence. Against a truly capable adversary Taylor might have gotten into serious trouble. As things turned out, however, he compiled a gleaming war record that eventually carried him into the White House.

Although the United States had a larger population than Mexico (17 million as opposed to 7 million) and was far more developed economically, the Mexican government at first believed it held the upper hand. After all, its regular army of 32,000 handily outnumbered the American army of just

In the Battle of Palo Alto, one of the first engagements of the Mexican War, U.S. field artillery proved especially potent at breaking up enemy charges and ensuring an American victory.

8,000. Its foot soldiers were trained in the best Napoleonic tradition and its light cavalry was among the best in the world. Mexican generalship, however, tended to be mediocre and the Mexican supply system was never very good. Fractious political infighting plagued the Mexicans throughout the struggle. And although the American army was usually outnumbered in the field, it was well-equipped and could draw upon a much bigger manpower base. It also possessed superb field artillery, an advantage it drew upon often.

The first major engagements occurred in May 1846, when 4,000 men under General Mariano Arista crossed the Rio Grande near its mouth, intent on thrashing the American upstarts at once. At the Battle of Palo Alto on May 8 he sent his infantry charging into Taylor's lines while his cavalry tried to turn the Americans' flanks. Taylor's artillery, however, crushed these attacks; the American infantry, for the most part, was never seriously engaged. The following day Taylor and Arista clashed again at Resaca de la Palma. Once more the Mexican army was beaten with heavy losses. Mexican casualties in the two battles exceeded 1,600 men; the Americans, by contrast, lost fewer than 200.

Nine days later Taylor crossed the Rio Grande and took possession of Matamoros, where he received substantial reinforcements and awaited instructions from the Polk administration. Eventually it was decided that he should capture Monterrey, the provincial capital of Nuevo León. After restaging his army to Camargo, Taylor began his offensive in August. One month later, having covered the intervening 125 miles, he fought a grueling three-day battle for Monterrey that bled his army heavily. When his opponent offered to yield the town in exchange for an eight-week armistice, Taylor agreed, much to Polk's baffled fury when he learned of the arrangement. The president promptly ordered Taylor to abrogate the truce and resume hostilities. Taylor complied and marched onward to Saltillo, the capital of Coahuila. Meanwhile another American column advanced through the province of Chihuahua. The end of 1846 found the United States firmly in control of much of northern Mexico as well as the coveted regions of California and New Mexico.

The Polk administration had calculated that the Mexican government should sue for peace at this point. It did nothing of the kind. Instead it redoubled its efforts under the charismatic leadership of General Santa Anna, the same man who had conceded Texas independence a decade earlier. Santa Anna was slippery and shrewd. When the war broke out, he had been living in exile in Cuba, a victim of Mexico's near-constant political turmoil. He sent word to Polk that if allowed to return to his homeland he would be willing to negotiate a swift end to the war. Polk therefore instructed the navy to give him safe conduct through its blockade of the Mexican coast. Once ashore, however, Santa Anna trumpeted that he had arrived to save the nation from American imperialism. He soon regained command of Mexico's army and by December 1846 had become president as well.

Early in 1847 it became apparent to Santa Anna that the Americans were planning a new offensive, this one apparently aimed at the coastal port of Veracruz. He also learned that many of Taylor's troops in northern Mexico had been diverted for this new operation. Accordingly, Santa Anna moved north at the head of 20,000 men, hoping to destroy Taylor's force and then swing eastward to defend Veracruz. After a remarkable 200-mile march across desert terrain, Santa Anna confronted the Americans at Buena Vista, just south of Saltillo. Although he had lost a full quarter of his strength in the rapid approach march, he still had 15,000 men to hurl against Taylor's 5,000.

Taylor had assumed the Mexicans could not march an army across such barren country to attack him. But he gamely withdrew a few miles into a naturally strong position near a hacienda called Buena Vista and there awaited the enemy attack. This position—a latticework of hills and ravines—partially nullified the Mexicans' numerical advantage. Even so, Santa Anna hurled his troops forward with great determination. For two days (February 22–23), the battle raged; and on several occasions the American line nearly broke. But Taylor shuttled his troops from one threatened point to another and each time the Americans managed to hold. A particularly crucial ingredient in the American defense was their magnificent field artillery. Without it, one U.S. general remarked, "we could not have maintained our position a single hour." Finally Santa Anna withdrew, having lost 2,000 men killed and wounded. American losses were fewer—about 750—but greater in proportion to the number of troops engaged.

Although Buena Vista sealed "Old Rough and Ready's" reputation and helped vault him into the White House, it was, in many respects, a needless battle. The advanced position held by the Americans was of little strategic value; a better defense could have been made at Monterrey. By electing

General Winfield Scott epitomized the incipient professionalism of the American officer corps in the mid-nineteenth century. His campaign against Mexico City in 1847 was a masterpiece.

to fight at Buena Vista, Taylor risked a disastrous reversal that might have prolonged the war indefinitely.

Scott's 1847 Campaign

While Taylor fought at Buena Vista, a new campaign was beginning along the Mexican coast. Commanded by the U.S. Army's general-in-chief, Winfield Scott, this campaign was aimed at capturing the port of Veracruz on the Gulf of Mexico and then marching inland against Mexico City. With the enemy's capital in American hands, it was believed, Mexican political life would be paralyzed and the Mexicans forced to the conference table.

Thus far, American operations in the war had been characterized by much the same amateurishness as in the War of 1812, notwithstanding their much greater success. Scott's campaign, however, was a masterpiece from beginning to end and displayed considerable thought in planning as well as audacity in execution. A new level of professionalism was on display at Veracruz, where Scott's troops made a well-synchronized landing in surf boats designed expressly for the purpose. Moreover, the fleet of transports had been carefully "combat-loaded," to use a twentieth-century term, so that the items needed first were stored so that they would be the first to be unloaded. The Mexicans chose not to oppose this landing, but even had they done so the Americans would probably still have prevailed, thanks to Scott's meticulous preparations.

Veracruz fell after a brief siege. In April, Scott's army began its advance inland. Ahead of them lay Santa Anna who, with his usual energy, had hustled back from northern Mexico and assembled another army of about 25,000 to confront this new American offensive. Forty miles inland

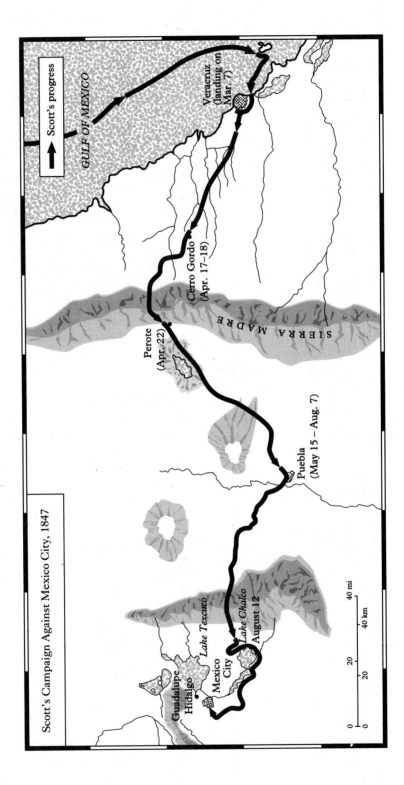

Scott's Campaign Against Mexico City, 1847

GULF OF MEXICO

→ Scott's progress

Veracruz (landing on Mar. 7)

Cerro Gordo (Apr. 17–18)

SIERRA MADRE

Perote (Apr. 22)

Puebla (May 15 – Aug. 7)

Lake Texcuco

Guadalupe Hidalgo

Mexico City

Lake Chalco
August 12

40 mi

40 km

0   20   20   40

0

the highway from the coast to Mexico City ascended rapidly into the mountains of the Sierra Madre. At a place called Cerro Gordo the Mexican commander elected to make his stand. The position seemed impassable; Scott, however, sent his engineers to locate a path around it and, when one was found, sent an infantry division on a circuitous march around the Mexican left flank and rear, turning the main line of defense. After a sharp little fight, Santa Anna's army fell back in disorder. Scott continued another twelve miles to Jalapa.

At Jalapa the essentially amateur nature of the American military establishment reasserted itself. Seven regiments of Scott's troops were twelve-month volunteers whose enlistments were about to expire. Most flatly refused to reenlist, and Scott had no choice but to let them march back to the coast and board ships back to the United States. At about the same time, realizing that the yellow-fever season would soon grip the lowlands, he withdrew most of the garrisons linking him with Veracruz. Then in August he continued his advance inland. He was now down to just 11,000 troops and had no dependable line of communication. The venerable Duke of Wellington, told of this development, is supposed to have declared flatly, "Scott is lost. . . . He can't take [Mexico] city, and he can't fall back upon his base."

But Scott proved the duke wrong. Husbanding his troops with great care, he masterfully kept up his offensive through a series of adroit maneuvers. His operations generally followed the pattern set at Cerro Gordo. The Mexicans would establish a seemingly impregnable defensive position, but young American officers would reconnoiter tirelessly until they found an unguarded path through or around the Mexican lines. In this fashion, Scott's army advanced within a few miles of the capital.

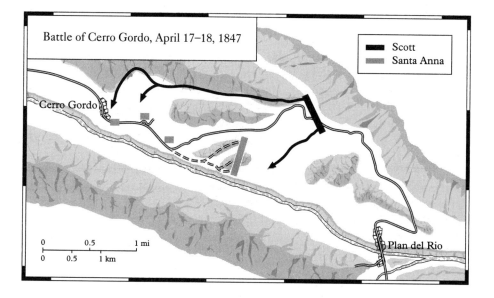

Battle of Cerro Gordo, April 17–18, 1847

Scott
Santa Anna

Cerro Gordo

Plan del Rio

| 0 | 0.5 | 1 mi |
| 0 | 0.5 | 1 km |

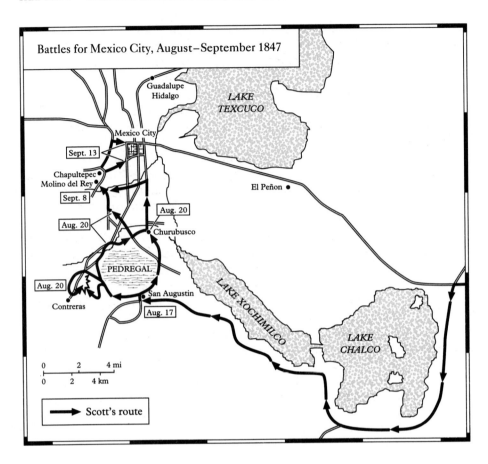

Battles for Mexico City, August–September 1847

The final assaults on Mexico City displayed the American army at its doughty best. Each operation typically began with a careful reconnaissance by engineer officers who probed the enemy lines for weaknesses and generally found them. The terrain was a rough network of hills, marshes, and rock-strewn fields, but Mexican defenders tended to overestimate its difficulty. When told, for example, that American artillery was picking its way through a solidified lava bed called the Pedregal, one Mexican officer laughed. "No! No! You're dreaming, man. The birds couldn't cross that Pedregal." Only when solid shot began to rain on his position did he realize his error.

As the anecdote suggests, American cannoneers often placed their light fieldpieces at the forefront of the fighting. Artillery typically opened an offensive engagement, where its fire helped neutralize enemy cannon, demoralize the defenders, and embolden friendly foot soldiers. When the infantrymen attacked, they tended to work their away around the Mexican flank or exploit gaps in the defenses. Only occasionally did they resort to a frontal attack. When they did, however, severe casualties could result. At the Battle of Molino del Rey, for example, the American division that made the assault lost 25 percent of its strength in a few hours of fighting. But the U.S. troops had formed the habit of winning, so that even when good tactical sense was lacking, their self-confidence and élan prevailed. When the formidable castle of Chapultepec—a key to the defense of Mexico City—fell to the Americans, a stunned Santa Anna remarked, "I believe if we were to plant our batteries in Hell the damned Yankees would take them from us." But although impressive, these American triumphs were ultimately misleading, for they occurred where the enemy possessed smoothbore muskets and artillery. They gave American officers an exaggerated view of the frontal assault's potential. During the Civil War to come, such attacks against rifled muskets and artillery often resulted only in expensive failure.

On September 14, 1847, Scott's army entered the Mexican capital. They had achieved a remarkable success. With fewer than 11,000 troops, the Americans had overcome a force of 30,000, well-entrenched and fighting on the defensive, and killed, wounded, or made prisoner a number of Mexican soldiers equal to Scott's entire army. Nominally the Mexican army remained intact. But just as Scott had predicted, the seizure of the capital so paralyzed Mexican political life that within a few weeks, the Mexicans opened negotiations for peace. The resulting Treaty of Guadalupe-Hidalgo was signed in February 1848. Under its terms, the Americans received Texas (with its boundary stipulated as the Rio Grande) and also gained California and New Mexico. In exchange the United States assumed the claims of American citizens against the Mexican government and also paid Mexico $15 million.

The Americans also gained an unexpected political nightmare. The question of whether the newly acquired territories would be slave or free haunted the nation for the next decade; it eventually exploded into civil war. Ulysses S. Grant, who considered the Mexican War "one of the most unjust ever waged by a stronger against a weaker nation," would see in this a bitter justice. "Nations, like individuals, are punished for their transgressions," he would note in his memoirs. "We got our punishment in the most sanguinary and expensive war of modern times."

The Mexican War was the first successful American attempt to project a major force beyond their own boundaries. The navy played a role similar to that of Great Britain's navy in the American Revolution: it permitted U.S. forces to move at will and to remain, for the most part, in continuous supply. By and large, both American regulars and volunteers performed well. The United States proved able to mobilize and maintain forces over a long period and at considerable distance from American soil.

On the American side, about 30,000 regular officers and men served in the war. Of these, 7,700 died—about 900 in battle, the rest from disease. About 73,000 volunteer officers and men enlisted, but many never left the United States. Of those who did, 607 were killed (most in Taylor's dubious battle at Buena Vista); another 6,400 died of disease.

Most senior American officers turned in the same uneven performance characteristic of previous American wars. The young, West Point–trained officers, however, displayed a consistent military competence rarely seen before. They thus bore testimony to a still-underdevoped but growing military professionalism. Winfield Scott, of course, was the outstanding military strategist of the war—one might say the only real strategist. Yet ironically Taylor, not Scott, became the next president, although Scott made his own bid for the White House in 1852.

The Mexican War is often considered a "dress rehearsal" for the Civil War. It certainly gave many future Civil War commanders experience. But it was really more like a well-fought War of 1812. The armies were still quite limited in size—Scott's entire army, by Civil War standards, would scarcely have made a respectable army corps. Both sides used predominantly smoothbore muskets and cannon with ranges and performance little different from those of the eighteenth century. The objectives of the Mexican War and Civil War were also quite dissimilar. While the Civil War was, in most respects, a total war fought for sheer national survival, the Mexican War was essentially a limited war fought in a manner not terribly different from the dynastic wars of eighteenth-century Europe. Limited in geographic setting, limited in allocation of resources, limited in immediate domestic impact and on the enemy's own political and social system, it bore little resemblance to the cataclysm whose origins it inadvertently sowed.

Technological Adaptation and Strategic Thought

That greater catastrophe, however, lay years in the future. In the meantime the American military congratulated itself on its victory, basked in a brief moment of glory, and then returned to its usual work of policing the now greatly expanded frontier. Discouraged by their colorless peacetime duties, a number of American officers left the service during the 1850s and sought more lucrative employment with the railroads, banks, and mining concerns that grew with the booming economy. Those who remained, however, continued the twin tasks of professionalizing the armed forces and trying to keep pace with the fast-moving technological currents of the day. Their achievements would greatly affect the conduct of the massive conflict now looming, unseen and only dimly felt, just beyond the political horizon.

New Technologies

Arriving in New York harbor in 1861, a visiting Frenchman was charmed by a calliope cheerfully piping away from the fantail of a nearby steamboat. That this novel instrument used steam to make music struck the Frenchman as both charming and appropriate. "The grateful Americans," he wrote, "have introduced that powerful agent of their fortune everywhere and even admit it into the realm of art." It was an apt comment, for no technological force exerted a greater effect on nineteenth-century America than that protean brainchild of James Watt, the steam engine.

This "agent of fortune" had two main incarnations. On water, steamboats freed vessels from the tyranny of wind and currents. On land, smoke-belching railroad trains sent dozens of passengers and tons of freight hurtling along at speeds (25 to 50 miles per hour) that seemed to annihilate distance. Taken together, these two forms of steam transportation battered down the geographical barriers to trade and increasingly brought Americans within the orbit of a single, nationwide market. Their economic value was obvious, their military importance scarcely less so. From the 1820s onward, American soldiers and sailors spent a great deal of time pondering the potentialities of steam power.

The steamboat came first. John Fitch constructed a working steam vessel as early as 1789, and by 1807 Robert Fulton's famous *Clermont* was plying the Hudson River. Seven years later, Fulton built the world's first steam warship to defend New York harbor against British attack. The potential military advantages of such a warship were considerable. It could go anywhere, heedless of adverse wind patterns or periods of calm. It could enter harbors and rivers more easily and thus held special promise for inshore operations against forts. The disadvantages, however, initially seemed daunting. Chief among these were the huge cost of the engines; the reduced cruising radius when using engines; the myriad complications from maintenance problems and coal sources; and the decreased working and living space for the crew, made necessary by the sheer bulk of the steam engines.

The drawbacks did not end there. Steam power was at first quite inefficient, requiring huge quantities of fuel in exchange for comparatively

A splendid example of the U.S. Navy's new generation of steam-powered warships, the USS *Merrimac* was also a fully rigged sailing vessel, partly as an economy measure, partly as insurance in case of mechanical failure. Although scuttled at the outbreak of the Civil War, it was salvaged by the Confederates and converted into the ironclad CSS *Virginia*.

little useful work. The development in 1837 of a high-pressure, reciprocal engine eased this problem a bit, but steam vessels remained energy hogs—particularly in comparison with elegant, inexpensive wind-powered sailing ships. There was also the matter of the huge paddlewheel that propelled the steam vessel through the water. Not only did it dramatically reduce the number of cannon that a warship could mount, the paddlewheel was highly vulnerable to enemy fire. The obvious alternative, the screw propeller, raised technological problems that took time to solve. Not until 1843 did the American navy launch its first propeller-driven warship, the *Princeton*. With its introduction the navy at last had a steam-powered warship that could fully compete with its wind-driven counterpart. But even then the problem of greater expense remained.

A major improvement in naval artillery also occurred during the 1850s. Commander John A. Dahlgren—chief of ordnance at the Washington Navy Yard from 1847 to 1861 (when he became its commandant)—tirelessly sought to develop large but safe shell-firing guns. Eventually he hit upon a durable design—an 11-inch muzzle-loading smoothbore weapon with a distinctive "coke bottle" shape to absorb gunpowder blast. It could fire either solid shot or shell. Shells could splinter the hull of a wooden warship in a way solid shot could not, while solid shot remained useful for duels against shore fortifications. Dahlgren's invention became an important intermediate step between the old-style smoothbore cannon from the days of Nelson and the high-velocity rifled artillery of the future.

The Dahlgren gun also signaled a trend toward mounting fewer but larger guns aboard warships, a trend driven in part by the growing use of steam engines aboard warships. The marriage of steam and ordnance involved a major trade-off as increases in engine size forced reductions in the space available for guns. During this period of transition in naval technology, developing an optimal design for warships proved difficult. The notion of protecting warships with iron plates further complicated the problem. Both Great Britain and France experimented with such "ironclad" vessels, but the United States initially held back. Not until the Civil War would Americans construct armored warships.

On land the army also grappled with the implications of steam and improved ordnance. To be sure, the navy's harnessing of steam power had no exact counterpart in the army. The War Department neither constructed special military trains nor commissioned studies—as did the Prussian general staff—to think systematically about the possible use of railroads in national defense. Nevertheless, inspired by its role in the republic as an important surveyor of potential railroad routes, the War Department did sponsor a number of engineering studies that dealt with such technical matters as track gradients, the design of suspension systems, and so on. Although little was directly related to warfare, such studies gave many engineering officers a close acquaintance with the demands and potentialities of the railroad. When the Civil War came, as a result, most commanders possessed a fairly good understanding of railroads and were quick to exploit this new means of transportation.

By 1860, however, steam warships had not replaced the sailing navy, nor had the railroad eclipsed the army wagon. All steam vessels remained fully equipped with masts, sails, and rigging for purposes of fuel economy or the likely event of engine failure. And where railroad tracks ended, men and supplies still had to be transported by water or, more usually, by teams of horses. Civil War armies typically needed about one draft horse for every two or three soldiers.

Technological innovation also occurred in the realm of army ordnance. Two deceptively simple advances in the realm of small arms contributed heavily to the carnage of the Civil War. The first of these was the percussion cap, the latest advance in the continuing quest to touch off a powder charge with greater reliability. Essentially a small brass fitting with a daub of mercury fulminate painted on the inside, it could be fitted snugly over a nipple at the breach of the weapon; the nipple had a small hole that provided access to the powder charge. When the weapon's hammer fell, it struck the percussion cap with enough force to ignite the mercury fulminate, send a spark into the chamber, and ignite the powder charge. The used cap could then be quickly discarded and a new one emplaced for the next firing. The percussion-cap system dispensed with the need to prime the weapon and achieved a much lower rate of misfire than the flintlock system that had been in use since the seventeenth century. During the Mexican War the American regular army largely eschewed the new-fangled percussion cap, but less hide-bound volunteer units used it widely. By the 1850s the army had adopted this system, and it was in general use during the Civil War.

The other significant advance was the creation of the first truly practical rifled musket. For centuries marksmen had understood that a projectile that spiraled in flight went farther and more accurately than a projectile that did not. The trick, of course, was to put spiral grooves in the barrel that would impart the desired spinning motion. For the grooves to achieve their effect, however, the projectile needed to "grip" the barrel snugly, a requirement that created significant military problems.

Model 1855 Rifled Musket. Civil War rifled muskets employed two new technologies: the percussion cap, which reduced the number of misfires; and the Minié ball, a bullet that enabled rifles to be loaded as rapidly as smoothbores. The result was an unprecedented extension in range and accuracy that transformed the battlefield.

With a smoothbore musket one could simply pour some powder down the barrel and then drop in the bullet, a process that took very little time. With a rifled musket, however, one had to pound the bullet down the barrel with a mallet and a long rod. All that pounding took time. Meanwhile, an enemy armed with a smoothbore musket could hurry forward and shoot first. That was why armies in the eighteenth and early nineteenth centuries mainly used smoothbores. Only special troops used rifles.

In the 1840s, however, a French army captain, Claude E. Minié, invented a way to load a rifled musket as easily as a smoothbore. Called the "Minié ball," it was a cylindro-conoidal bullet that could be dropped right down the barrel. One end of it was hollow. When the rifle was fired, the expanding gas made by the gunpowder widened the sides of this hollow end, and the sides of the hollow end gripped the rifling, creating the spinning effect required for good accuracy. Instead of hitting a target at a maximum of one hundred yards, a good marksman could hit a target with a rifled musket at four times that range or better.

Spurred by the energetic Jefferson Davis, who served as secretary of war in the mid-1850s, the army quickly adopted the rifled musket. It also pondered how to modify its infantry tactics to adapt to this innovation. The fruit of these ruminations, however, amounted to little more than an increase in the regulation marching pace of soldiers on the attack. They must reach the enemy line more rapidly, it was understood, to compensate for the increased range and accuracy of the rifled musket. No one yet guessed what thousands of Minié balls—deadly at ranges of 400 yards and beyond—could really do to troops advancing shoulder-to-shoulder in the old Napoleonic style. As is usual (and quite understandable) in such situations, military men expected that this new development would simply modify the existing tactical environment, not overthrow it.

American Military Thought

Few American officers during the 1850s gave extended attention to the problems of conducting a major war. Most were too busy fighting Indians, angling for promotion, or simply enduring a life of monotonous garrison duty. As future Confederate General Richard S. Ewell remarked, before the Civil War he learned everything there was to know about commanding fifty dragoons and forgot about everything else. Still, some officers did think seriously about strategic matters. And since most of these rose to high rank during the Civil War, their efforts leavened the indifference of their peers and, in fact, gave the conduct of that war a surprising degree of coherence. Like soldiers the world over, these more industrious American officers had to grapple with the legacy of Napoleon. But they also had to consider the military realities of defending a nation with only a small standing army and one that was, after all, separated from any major enemy by 3,000 miles of ocean.

The dean of American strategic thinkers was Dennis Hart Mahan, professor of military science at West Point. A deep admirer of Napoleon, Mahan saw this great captain chiefly through the eyes of the Swiss military theorist Antoine Henri, Baron de Jomini. Jomini emphasized the offensive essence of Napoleonic warfare but gave it an orderly, geometric cast. Similarly, Mahan celebrated the aggressive pursuit of offensive victory but lavished even greater attention upon the problems of defense. Recognizing that, in the event of war, many American soldiers would be half-trained volunteers, Mahan dwelled heavily on using field fortifications to steady new troops and reduce casualties. His ideal was the active defense—to weaken and absorb the enemy's blow, then "when he has been cut up, to assume the offensive, and drive him back at the point of the bayonet."

During his many years at West Point, Mahan drilled his ideas into a generation of cadets and presided over a "Napoleon Club" that studied the emperor's campaigns. His principal disciple, Henry Wager Halleck, translated Jomini's principal works into English and also wrote a somewhat derivative study entitled *Elements of Military Art and Science* (1846). Halleck solemnly extolled not only the virtues of field fortification but also the imperative need to keep one's forces well concentrated and vigilant against surprise attack.

Although never adopted as a West Point text, Halleck's book was probably the strategic treatise most widely read by American officers. But that is not really saying a great deal. Few references to Jomini or formal strategic theory appear in Civil War correspondence, and successful Civil War commanders often regarded their strategy as a matter of applied common sense. As Grant remarked of Napoleon, "[M]y impression is that his first success came because he made war in his own way, and not in imitation of others."

After the Mexican War the U.S. War Department sent a number of officers abroad in an effort to keep abreast of recent European military developments. But the results were not impressive. For example, a trio of officers sent to study the armies of Europe returned to make a bulky but uneven report. From their observations of the Crimean War they commented learnedly on the leggings used by Russian soldiers but failed to say anything about the Russian conscription system. American officers did better when they left the higher realms of military policy and pondered more workaday issues instead. A number of them wrote military manuals or prepared articles on technical aspects of the military profession. Some discussed better ways to train infantry, others offered suggestions on the improvement of cannon, saddles, firearms, and other items of equipment. One historian has argued that in this respect, antebellum officers were at least as professionally active as their late-twentieth-century counterparts.

＊　　＊　　＊　　＊

By the eve of the Civil War, the United States had created a modest but reasonably proficient military establishment. Although its regular army numbered just 16,000 men in 1860, the limited standing force was adequate to perform the duties of a "frontier constabulary," and, supplemented by short-term volunteers, it had handily prevailed over a numerically larger opponent during the Mexican War. Moreover, Americans had also created a substantial system of permanent fortifications to guard their coastline.

American forces had also kept abreast of technological improvements. On land, army officers understood the importance of railroads and were well prepared to exploit that new means of transportation during the Civil War. They had also adopted the rifled musket and had attempted, however imperfectly, to anticipate its effect on infantry tactics. At sea, the navy possessed steam warships of advanced design and had also deployed new, state-of-the-art naval guns.

Perhaps most impressively, in the years after the War of 1812 the officer corps took the first significant steps toward true professional status. The U.S. Military Academy, although established in 1802, came into its own with the Thayer reforms of the 1820s. Officers increasingly viewed the military profession as a lifelong career, and a sizable number of them thought seriously about the military art. When the vicissitudes of Congress permitted, they even established schools of practice to train more thoroughly in infantry and artillery tactics.

Yet substantial problems lingered. In the years after the War of 1812 the militia system steadily declined. The presence of some peacetime volunteer companies and the enlistment of additional volunteers in wartime only partially offset the endemic shortage of trained military manpower. A strong amateur tradition also persisted. Most Americans continued to believe that an intelligent man of character, imbued with martial enthusiasm and fired by republican ideals, could make not only a good soldier but also a competent officer. Among its many other effects on American society, the Civil War would mortally challenge this belief.

SUGGESTED READINGS

Bauer, K. Jack. *The Mexican War, 1846–1848* (New York: MacMillan, 1974).

Coffman, Edward M. *The Old Army: A Portrait of the American Army in Peacetime, 1784–1898* (New York and London: Oxford University Press, 1986).

Crackel, Theodore. *Mr. Jefferson's Army: Political and Social Reform of the Military Establishment, 1801–1809* (New York and London: New York University Press, 1987).

Cunliffe, Marcus. *Soldiers and Civilians: The Martial Spirit in America, 1775–1865* (New York: Free Press, 1968).

Hickey, Don. *The War of 1812: A Forgotten Conflict* (Urbana: University of Illinois Press, 1989).

Kohn, Richard H. *Eagle and Sword: The Beginnings of the Military Establishment in America* (New York: Free Press, 1975).

McCaffrey, James M. *Army of Manifest Destiny: The American Soldier in the Mexican War, 1846–1848* (New York and London: New York University Press, 1992).

McKee, Christopher. *A Gentlemanly and Honorable Profession: The Creation of the U.S. Naval Officer Corps* (Annapolis: Naval Institute Press, 1991).

Mahon, John D. *History of the Second Seminole War* (Gainesville: University Presses of Florida, 1968).

Morrison, James L., Jr. *"The Best School in the World": West Point, the Pre–Civil War Years, 1835–1866* (Kent, Ohio: Kent State University Press, 1986).

Prucha, Francis P. *The Sword of the Republic: The United States Army on the Frontier, 1783–1846* (New York: MacMillan, 1969).

Skelton, William B. *An American Profession of Arms: The Army Officer Corps, 1784–1861* (Lawrence: University Press of Kansas, 1992).

Smith, Merritt Roe. *Harper's Ferry and the New Technology* (Ithaca, N.Y.: Cornell University Press, 1977).

Stagg, J. C. A. *Mr. Madison's War: Politics, Diplomacy, and Warfare in the Early American Republic, 1783–1830* (Princeton, N.J.: Princeton University Press, 1983).

Utley, Robert M. *Frontiersmen in Blue: The United States Army and the Indian, 1848–1865* (New York: MacMillan, 1967).

2

THE CIVIL WAR, 1861-1862:
THE LETHAL FACE OF BATTLE

Strategic Overview

War for the Borderland

Cracking the Confederate
Frontier

At 4:30 A.M. on April 12, 1861, a dull boom thudded across the tranquil harbor of Charleston, South Carolina. From the city, observers could clearly see the fuse of a mortar shell as it climbed across the soft moonlit sky, then plunged in a graceful arc toward casemated Fort Sumter near the harbor entrance. A moment later the shell exploded directly above the fort, raining fragments on the federal garrison below. The Civil War—the deadliest conflict in American history and, in many respects, the central episode of that history—had begun.

No one had any idea what to expect. Most Americans supposed the war would be decided by one or two major battles. A few even believed it might end without any serious fighting at all. But nearly everyone agreed that, at most, the struggle would be settled within a year. They also assumed that the fundamental patterns of American society would remain unaltered. Indeed, the preservation of those patterns formed the very object for which Americans on both sides were contending. White Southerners expected to maintain an agrarian, slave-holding society that, in their minds at least, corresponded to the republic established by the Founding Fathers. Northerners sought to restore the unbroken alliance of states toasted by President Andrew Jackson nearly three decades before ("Our Federal Union—it must be preserved!").

But instead of a brief contest, the Civil War raged across the central and southern United States for four long years. And instead of conserving the old America—however defined—it steadily and profoundly reshaped the political, economic, and social contours of the nation. By the time it ended, the original American republic was gone forever.

The Civil War was, as one historian has aptly called it, "the Second

American Revolution." Like the War for Independence, it was a revolutionary conflict, combining the mass politics and passions of the wars of the French Revolution with the technology, productive capacity, and managerial style of an emergent industrial society. Both the Union and the Confederacy fielded armies that dwarfed all military formations previously seen in the New World. They supplied these vast hosts with food, munitions, and equipment shipped by rail and steamship. They connected units hundreds of miles apart with webs of telegraph lines, and motivated soldiers and civilians alike with ceaseless barrages of political propaganda. When necessary they repressed dissent with intimidation and arbitrary arrests. Before the war was half over, both sides abandoned cherished notions of individual liberty and conscripted men to serve in the armies. In their quest to finance the struggle they trampled venerable ideas about limited taxation and fiscal rectitude. And by the war's third year they had begun to accept attacks upon enemy civilians and property as necessary and even virtuous. Both sides mobilized their resources and populations to the utmost limit of their mid-nineteenth-century ability and, when they reached the end of that ability, strove for ways to extend it. The Union and the Confederacy, in short, waged a total war: a war in which both societies pitted their full destructive energies against each other.

Strategic Overview

To understand the course of the war, one must understand its origins, for perceptions concerning the roots of the conflict profoundly shaped the objectives and strategy of both sides. The central issue was slavery, although many Americans did not accept this at the time (and some still do not today). One alternative view suggests that the Civil War was a struggle over "states' rights" versus centralized government—yet most Northerners believed in states' rights as much as most Southerners. Another regards it as a contest between an agrarian South and an industrialized North, neglecting to note that the Northern states were also primarily agricultural—in the case of the midwest, overwhelmingly so. Still another posits a conflict between two allegedly distinct cultures—overlooking the fact that North and South shared a common language, a common history, and a common belief in republican government. Such political, economic, and cultural differences as did exist could be traced, by and large, to a single source: the fact that the South was a slaveholding society and the North was not.

Roots of War

By the mid-nineteenth century, slavery had become the South's bedrock institution. In the 250 years since the first shackled Africans had arrived on American shores (and especially in the decades following the American

Revolution), white Southerners had evolved a complex set of beliefs about their "peculiar institution." Not only did they consider it vital for the cultivation of the region's major cash crops, they also thought it the only acceptable basis on which whites and blacks could coexist. Slaveholders liked to regard their bondsmen essentially as children incapable of self-improvement and therefore in need of their master's lifelong paternal care. Many believed—or affected to believe—that the blacks themselves preferred a life of slavery and benefited from it. Paradoxically most Southerners also possessed a profound if usually unstated fear of a slave revolt. The need to maintain absolute, unquestioned control over their slave population gave Southerners a strong incentive to preserve an ordered, stable society. As a result, social change of any kind occurred in the South more slowly than in the North. And although only one in four Southern families actually owned slaves, most accepted the proslavery philosophy. They either aspired to ownership or, at a minimum, appreciated the advantages of living in a society whose lowest tier remained permanently reserved for blacks.

Northerners, however, increasingly found the "peculiar institution" distasteful. Comparatively little of this distaste reflected humanitarian concern for the slaves. Perhaps 5 percent of the Northern population entertained "abolitionist" sentiments: that is to say, a belief in both immediate, uncompensated emancipation *and* political and social equality for blacks. The vast majority of antislavery Northerners objected to the "peculiar institution" not because of its effect on black people, but because of its effect on whites. It degraded the value of free labor. It encouraged an agrarian society dominated by a comparative handful of wealthy planters who (many believed) monopolized political power in the South. Conversely it discouraged the creation of new industry and economic diversity. And to the extent that slavery was permitted in the western territories, it meant that white families would be forced to live beside blacks, a prospect that many Northern whites considered repugnant.

Until the late 1840s this tension between pro- and antislavery forces remained largely submerged. It surfaced rapidly when the Mexican War broke out. Many Whigs and some Northern Democrats regarded the conflict as nothing but a naked land grab by Southern slaveholders eager to extend slavery into Mexico. In August 1846 antislavery congressman David Wilmot of Pennsylvania introduced a resolution that formally renounced any intention by the United States to introduce slavery into any lands that might be seized from Mexico during the war. This "Wilmot Proviso" failed to pass both houses of Congress, but it succeeded in reinjecting slavery into national political life. For the next fifteen years the question of slavery in the territories constantly dogged American policy makers.

At bottom, the question dividing Americans might be summarized thus: was the United States a slaveholding republic with pockets of freedom in the North, or was it a free republic with pockets of slavery in the South? The answer had profound implications for the very nature of the American experiment and its future. Proslavery Americans sought to extend slavery into the territories because they considered anything less to be an abridgment of their rights and an implicit query against the legitimacy of their way of life. Antislavery Americans wanted to bar the extension of slavery because they believed the system degraded the dignity of free labor and stifled economic diversity. More darkly, they suspected that the slave system sustained a planter aristocracy that controlled political life in the South and was trying to maintain control over national political life as well.

Throughout the 1850s, both sides saw evidence to support their own beliefs. Political compromise grew more difficult. An attempt to permit western settlers to decide for themselves whether a given territory would be slaveholding or free degenerated into violence when the rival factions in Kansas Territory undermined the democratic process through intimidation, fraud, and murder. Then in 1859 the abolitionist terrorist John Brown raided Harpers Ferry, Virginia, hoping to foment a slave insurrection. The operation was a fiasco; Brown was captured and hanged, as were most of his followers who survived the attack itself. But the Harpers Ferry raid shocked the entire white population of the South, especially when they discovered that a few Northern abolitionists had helped finance Brown's attack. The fact that many in the North considered Brown a martyr only increased the Southerners' sense of anger and alienation.

For thirty years some Southerners had discussed the possibility of secession if the national government ever threatened the continued existence of slavery. The election of Republican candidate Abraham Lincoln seemed to bring that threat uncomfortably near. His party openly opposed the extension of slavery in the territories, and although Lincoln renounced any intention to touch slavery where it already existed, as president he would have power to appoint judges and federal marshals in the South. Such officials, indispensable to maintain the system of law and order on which slavery depended, would now be of dubious loyalty to the "peculiar institution." Perhaps most gallingly, Lincoln won election despite the fact that hardly any Southerners had voted for him. In most slaveholding states he had not even been on the ballot.

Many Southerners now sensed that they had lost control of the national government; they could no longer expect that government to preserve slavery. Honor and self-interest dictated that they must leave the Union if they expected to retain control of their own destinies. The secessionist impulse was particularly strong in South Carolina, a state in which slaves outnumbered whites and which had a long tradition of radicalism on the subject of slavery. On December 20, 1860, a convention of South Carolinians unanimously voted to leave the Union. Six other states followed in the next six weeks: Mississippi, Alabama, Louisiana, Georgia, Florida, and Texas. It was the worst crisis the nation had ever faced.

However, eight slave states—North Carolina, Tennessee, Virginia, Arkansas, Maryland, Kentucky, Missouri, and Delaware—remained loyal to the Union. This suggested that many Southerners did not wish to secede, an impression reinforced by the fact that in most of the states that *did* leave the Union, a substantial minority had voted against secession. For these and other reasons, when the Lincoln administration took office in March 1861, it hoped that some means might be found to undermine the secessionist

Perhaps America's greatest war president, Abraham Lincoln combined political skill with dogged determination and at times even ruthlessness.

movement without bloodshed. Perhaps, as Secretary of State William Seward believed, most Southerners would eventually repudiate disunion if given time to reconsider.

In the meantime, however, delegates from the seceded states formed a new nation, the Confederate States of America. Meeting in Montgomery, Alabama, they drafted a new constitution and established a provisional government to be led by Jefferson Davis, a former U.S. senator and secretary of war. One of the new government's first acts was to assume authority over the artillery batteries erected by South Carolina to threaten the tiny Federal garrison of Fort Sumter.

The Confederate government insisted that the Lincoln administration withdraw the garrison: its claim to sovereignty over the seceded South would be meaningless if a "foreign" power continued to occupy one of the Confederacy's principal ports. The symbolism of Fort Sumter was equally important to Lincoln, since to order its evacuation would be a fatal display of weakness. For weeks the standoff persisted. Finally President Davis gave orders that if the fort refused to surrender it must be bombarded. The firing on Fort Sumter on April 12 ended any chance the sectional rift could be repaired without bloodshed. Undermanned, low on food, and cut off from resupply, Fort Sumter surrendered on April 14. The following day Lincoln requested 75,000 three-month volunteers to suppress the rebellion.

Military Resources and Objectives

Lincoln's call for troops triggered a second wave of secession. The upper tier of southern states—Virginia, Arkansas, North Carolina, and Tennessee—all left the Union rather than support the North in a war against the Confederacy. By June the Confederacy consisted of eleven states, sprawling across a territory the size of western Europe and boasting a population of 9 million. Of these, about 5.5 million were whites. Most of the rest were slaves—a huge potential security problem, to be sure, but also a major economic asset.

The Confederacy's aim at the beginning of the war was simple: hold on to the de facto independence already obtained. It did not need to invade the North or dictate a peace treaty on the steps of the White House. All it had to do was to continue the struggle long enough for the North to tire of the war and accept the fact of secession. In many respects this aim was little different from that of the American colonies during the Revolution, a struggle still close enough in time to be almost a living memory. That earlier conflict had been won largely by attrition. The British had captured the colonies' cities almost at will, traversed American territory as they pleased, and dominated the seas that bathed American shores. But they could neither quench the Americans' will to fight nor prevent foreign intervention once the Americans had shown their capacity for sustained resistance.

Conceivably the Confederates might have adopted a similar strategy: pin their forces to the defense of no fixed area or city, draw the invaders in, and wear out the Federals by a protracted war of attrition. Instead Davis and his advisors decided to fight the battle at the frontier. They would repulse incursions and attempt to hold major concentrations of population and resources. A number of considerations made this the obvious strategy. First, the discrepancy in military strength between North and South, although hardly an even match, was far less forbidding than that between Britain and the American colonies. Second, the political pressures within the Confederacy for a conventional defense were also great—every locality clamored for Southern troops to protect it. Third, a conventional defense would give the Confederacy greater legitimacy in the eyes of its own citizens and in those of the world. And finally, the delicate "peculiar institution" needed the stability of law and order to survive. The mere presence of a hostile political party in the White House had threatened that stability enough to spur the cotton states to secession. Given the enormous sensitivity of this issue, the Confederacy could hardly permit Federal armies to plunge deep into Southern territory. Even if formal Federal policy remained one of non-interference with slave labor, an advancing Union army would surely disrupt slave labor, create a flood of runaways, and perhaps even raise the spectre of a race war of slave against master. The Confederacy, then, had many good reasons to defend itself at the border.

The South would not conduct a passive defense, either. Davis preferred what he called the "offensive-defensive." According to his scheme, Confederate forces would permit a Union thrust to develop, gauge its main axis of advance, wait for an advantageous moment, then concentrate and counterattack at a time and place of their own choosing. General Robert E.

Jefferson Davis was highly qualified to be the Confederacy's president, having been a Mexican War hero, Secretary of War in the Franklin Pierce administration, and a senator from Mississippi.

Lee described this operational concept in an 1863 letter: "It is [as] impossible for [the enemy] to have a large operating army at every assailable point in our territory as it is for us to keep one to defend it. We must move our troops from point to point as required, and by close observation and accurate information the true point of attack can generally be ascertained. . . . Partial encroachments of the enemy we must expect, but they can always be recovered, and any defeat of their large army will reinstitute everything."

Confederates worried comparatively little about the larger size and greater resource base of their opponent, partly from overconfidence, but primarily because of a conviction that the war would be brief and comparatively limited—a contest on the scale, say, of the recent Mexican War. But in a longer struggle the North's advantages were substantial. With a population of 20 million, the Northern states obviously possessed a much larger military manpower base, but their industrial capacity was far greater as well. In 1860 the North had over 110,000 manufacturing establishments, the South just 18,000. The North produced 94 percent of the country's iron, 97 percent of its coal and—not incidentally—97 percent of its firearms. It contained 22,000 miles of railroad to the South's 8,500. The North outperformed the South agriculturally as well. Northerners held 75 percent of the country's farm acreage, produced 60 percent of its livestock, 67 percent of its corn, and 81 percent of its wheat. All in all, they held 75 percent of the nation's total wealth.

The North's advantages did not end there. It controlled the resources of a long-established government, including the 16,000 men of its army and the ninety warships of its navy. It had a much better financial structure. The South, by contrast, had no preexisting armed forces, few banks, and relatively little specie. Its wealth lay primarily in land and slaves—assets difficult to convert to liquid capital. Shortly after the war began, the Confederate government made this deficiency even worse by ordering an embargo on the sale of cotton abroad. The decision, intended to pressure textile-producing nations like Great Britain into supporting the Confederacy, only hurt the South's ability to obtain more hard currency.

Even so, most of the North's advantages were potential rather than real. It would take time for the Union to translate its demographic and economic resources into effective strength, and in the interim the Confederacy would create military forces of impressive size. To be sure, the Federals usually held the edge in manpower and heavy weaponry, but only at the margins. And the South possessed considerable advantages of its own. Although the Union possessed more men, it also had the daunting task of projecting large armies across hundreds of miles of territory, much of it difficult to traverse and sparsely populated. Southern forces could rely upon a largely loyal population, whereas Union forces would have to divert large numbers of troops to guard supply lines and garrison key points against guerrilla incursions. Southern forces could fight on the defensive and exploit interior lines to concentrate against separate Union columns. Then too, the fact that Southerners were fighting to defend their homeland made their cause more concrete and thus more potent. Finally, with millions of slaves to keep the Southern economy running, the South could afford to send a larger percentage of its white manpower to war.

Of further benefit to the South was the fact that the Lincoln administration had to contend with an all-but-insoluble political conundrum. It had to maintain as broad a base of domestic support for the war as possible, despite the fact that some Northerners opposed any attempt to coerce the South, while many others believed the attempt must be made without trampling on the constitutional rights of Southerners—including their right to hold slaves. The administration also had to fight the war hard enough to gain victory but not so violently as to foster deep bitterness among the Southern people. The North's objective, after all, was a reunion of the states. If that were to be accomplished it required that the Southern people must eventually choose—grudgingly, perhaps, but essentially voluntarily—to renew their loyalty to the United States government. The dilemma facing the Lincoln administration was thus one of enormous complexity. It had to find a policy vigorous enough to win the war, but not so vigorous as to forfeit domestic support or alienate the South completely.

War for the Borderland

Nowhere was the Union task more delicate than in the borderland, a region consisting of Missouri, Kentucky, Maryland, and the western counties of

Virginia. These were slaveholding areas, each with considerable secessionist sentiment but also with substantial populations loyal to the Federal government. If the Lincoln administration could hold these areas, it stood a fighting chance of containing the rebellion. If, however, the Confederacy gained control of the borderland, it could isolate Washington, D.C., add another million people to its population, and render a Federal victory all but impossible. As both sides mobilized their field armies, they struggled first for control of the border states between them.

Mobilization

Since they shared an identical military heritage, it was scarcely surprising that the Union and Confederacy organized for war in similar ways. Lincoln, of course, had the advantage of preexisting War and Navy departments as well as small, permanent land and naval forces. But the Davis administration quickly created identical departments. In any event the United States prior to 1860 had no experience with a command structure adequate for the unprecedented size and scope of the conflict, and as a result both Davis and Lincoln had to experiment.

The paper organization Davis created was not bad. It combined a secretary of war with an adjutant and inspector general whom Davis expected would perform as a de facto chief of staff. In reality, however, Davis ran much of the war effort himself. The secretary of war position never amounted to much. The job passed from one man to another until the end of the Confederate government's existence. Davis apparently never sought, and certainly never found, a forceful and able secretary of war.

The Union command structure, although similar, had a few important differences. First, Lincoln wisely chose to invest his secretary of war with very wide powers. His initial choice for the position proved corrupt and inefficient, but in January 1862 Lincoln appointed a new man, Edwin M.

As Lincoln's Secretary of War, Edwin M. Stanton presided over a Union army of over one million men and kept it well supplied with arms and equipment.

Stanton of Pennsylvania, who became one of the most energetic and forceful secretaries of war in American history. "Stanton," Lincoln once remarked, "is the rock upon which are beating the waves of this conflict. . . . I do not see how he survives—why he is not crushed and torn to pieces. Without him, I should be destroyed." Lincoln also insisted—except for one brief interlude—on having a general-in-chief. During the course of the conflict he had four of them (Winfield Scott, George B. McClellan, Henry W. Halleck, and Ulysses S. Grant), and his experiences with all but the last were often frustrating. But by maintaining the post he prevented himself from becoming overwhelmed by detail and also, at least in theory, received the benefit of expert military advice.

Both sides spent the first months of the war feverishly generating armies far larger than any the United States had previously fielded. To do so, each mobilized its limited contingents of existing state militia, but these barely began to furnish the necessary manpower. To augment the militia, volunteer troops were enlisted by tens of thousands. In keeping with the traditional American political philosophy, chief responsibility for raising the volunteers reposed not with the central government but rather with the individual states. The Union and Confederate War departments simply asked each state to raise a certain number of regiments. The state governors, in turn, had the task of actually finding, organizing, and equipping the needed men. To do so they often turned to community leaders—men of established standing who could persuade other men to enlist under their command. Thus a prominent local attorney might announce that he was organizing a company of infantry. Other men, familiar with the attorney's reputation and willing to serve with him, would then enroll in the company until its rosters were filled. Afterward they would elect the key company officers and sergeants. The attorney, of course, would invariably be elected captain. The company would then band with other companies into a regiment, and the regiment's colonel would then be selected. Sometimes the governor would appoint him; sometimes he would be elected, if not by the rank and file then by the various company commanders. In this way the states met their quotas. The exact details varied widely but were always in keeping with the loose-jointed, localistic nature of American society.

In their homespun way, Americans were harnessing the same thing that had fired the French Revolution: popular sovereignty, the notion that the people themselves formed the ultimate source of political authority and legitimacy. Nowhere in the nineteenth-century world was this idea more potent than in the United States, and as a result both Northerners and Southerners felt a profound sense of identification with the cause for which their governments were contending. The gulf between the Civil War soldier and his eighteenth-century counterpart could hardly be more absolute. The old European soldier felt little sense of involvement with his sovereign's cause, nor did the peasants and burghers whose taxes paid for the war. By contrast, the Civil War soldier was a member of one of the most intensely politicized societies on earth. His sense of involvement with his cause—whether the cause of Union or the cause of Southern independence—was profound; the communities that sent him to war were equally so. The explosion of martial energy this produced in 1861 was as powerful as that of the French Revolution.

The consequences of popular sovereignty affected the Union and Confederate war efforts in other ways as well. For one thing, the improvised nature of the mobilization gave the state governors an enormous degree of importance and thus considerable influence. Two governors of particular note were Oliver Perry Morton of Indiana and Joseph G. Brown of Georgia. Morton took an almost proprietary interest in his Hoosier regiments and was known to complain vigorously whenever he believed they were being mishandled. He advanced or undercut the careers of several Union commanders. Brown, for his part, became the gadfly of the Davis administration, damned various administration policies, circumvented the operation of military conscription in his state, and often retained supplies and equipment for the use of Georgia troops alone.

Both sides also found it expedient to offer high military rank to important political figures. The Lincoln administration in particular tried to clinch the support of various Northern constituencies by making generals of favorite politicians. Thus Nathaniel P. Banks, former Speaker of the House, received a major general's commission to make sure that New England Democrats backed the Union war effort. Lincoln also made Franz Sigel a major general in order to secure the support of the German-American community. Students of the Civil War have long poured scorn upon these "political generals." But their derision reflects a fundamental misunderstanding of the military ethos that prevailed in mid-nineteenth-century America. A professional officer corps, in the modern sense of the term, hardly existed, and few Americans understood why it should. In the minds of many, the chief attributes of effective command were character and leadership ability, and surely any widely admired political figure possessed these. Such scorn also overlooks the fact that many of these "political generals" performed at least as well as some of their West Point–trained counterparts, while a few of them displayed genuine gifts.

As soon as these newly formed units could gather—erratically uniformed, gawky, ill-disciplined, but filled with ardor—they began to gravitate toward various points along the military frontier. Few of these movements occurred as the result of comprehensive planning on the part of the Union and Confederate high commands. No such planning had occurred; no overarching strategic vision existed on either side. Often a governor or department commander decided what places must be garrisoned or occupied as bases for subsequent advances. At this early stage, the war efforts of both North and South were very much improvised. Like the armies themselves, strategic decision-making was generally an ad hoc affair.

The Border States

Even so, both sides had evident priorities. The Confederacy positioned substantial forces to block the approaches to Richmond; the North, for its part, exerted almost frantic energies to ensure the safety of Washington. The

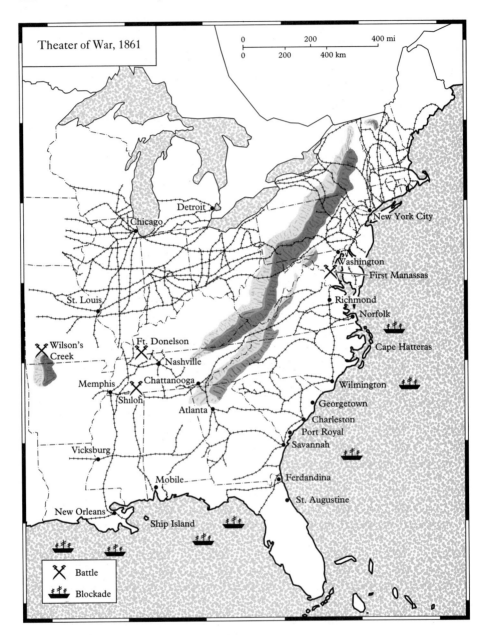

Theater of War, 1861

0   200   400 mi
0   200   400 km

Detroit
Chicago
New York City
Washington
First Manassas
St. Louis
Richmond
Norfolk
Cape Hatteras
Wilson's Creek
Ft. Donelson
Nashville
Memphis   Chattanooga
Shiloh
Atlanta
Wilmington
Georgetown
Charleston
Port Royal
Savannah
Vicksburg
Mobile
Ferdandina
New Orleans
Ship Island
St. Augustine

✕ Battle
⚓ Blockade

Federal capital was surrounded by slaveholding territory—Virginia, now part of a hostile power, lay just across the Potomac bridges, while Maryland hemmed in the District of Columbia on its remaining three sides. For a brief but terrifying moment it seemed likely that Maryland might leave the Union as well. Scant days after Fort Sumter, a secessionist mob had pelted Massachusetts troops as they marched through Baltimore en route to Washington; it was also widely rumored that the state legislature would shortly vote to join the Confederacy. The Maryland lawmakers never got the chance, however. Abandoning all concern for constitutional niceties, the

Lincoln administration suspended the writ of habeas corpus, declared martial law, imprisoned suspected persons, and in general clamped on Maryland a military despotism. This development was utterly startling in a nation long-wedded to the concept of limited government. It was also highly effective in keeping Maryland firmly within the Union—whether Marylanders liked it or not.

The Federal government enjoyed similar success in the western counties of Virginia. Economically this mountainous region was more tied to Ohio and Pennsylvania than to tidewater Virginia. It possessed relatively few slaves, a long tradition of resentment toward the more densely populated eastern counties, and considerable Unionist sentiment. In late May, when Federal troops from Ohio first crossed into western Virginia, they were widely received as liberators. The Confederacy had only a few weak units in the region, and those soon departed from the region after a series of minor clashes that nevertheless brought great results. The Federal victories in western Virginia secured Union control over the Baltimore and Ohio Railroad, a strategically invaluable artery between the eastern and western theaters of war. They also paved the way for the creation (in 1863) of the new state of West Virginia.

Kentucky, like western Virginia, was a state settled largely by Southerners but tied geographically and economically to the Ohio River valley. Perhaps not surprisingly, in the sectional squabbles that had preceded the war its citizens had exhibited a strong preference for compromise. The "Great Compromiser" himself, Senator Henry Clay, had been from Kentucky. So was Senator John J. Crittenden, principal proponent of a compromise proposal that had floated briefly during the secession winter. Nowhere was the "war of brothers" image more appropriate than in the Bluegrass State. Sixty percent of white Kentuckians who fought during the conflict wore Union blue; the rest wore gray. And in Kentucky the lines were indeed sometimes drawn within family circles. Crittenden had two sons who became generals on opposite sides.

When war broke out, Kentucky's governor tried in vain to mediate the conflict. When his efforts failed, the legislature voted that the state would maintain "strict neutrality." Lincoln, fearful that a tough policy would push Kentucky into the Confederate fold, gave orders to respect this extralegal neutrality. So did Davis. This anomalous situation lasted only until early September, when Confederate General Leonidas Polk—acting on his own authority—marched into Columbus, Kentucky. The town's position on a high bluff overlooking the Mississippi River gave it strategic value. By seizing Columbus, Polk strengthened the defense of the river, but the political cost was substantial. Although Federal troops (under Major General Ulysses S. Grant) promptly occupied other Kentucky towns at the mouths of the Cumberland and Tennessee rivers, the fact that the Confederacy had violated Kentucky neutrality first made it seem the aggressor. The state legislature embraced the Union; the prosecessionist governor resigned. By the end of the year Federal forces held most of the important points in Kentucky, including Louisville, the largest city, and Frankfort, the capital. The Confederates occupied only a thin strip along the state's southern frontier.

Missouri proved a thornier problem for the Lincoln administration. Although most of its citizens were pro-Union, a substantial minority favored the Confederates, and while Kentuckians adopted a largely neutral stance, the rival factions in Missouri quickly came to blows. Trouble began in mid-May when a mixed force of Union home guards and regulars marched into the camp of prosecessionist state militiamen and disarmed them. The Federal commander, Captain Nathaniel Lyon, had the captured militia herded through the streets of Saint Louis. An angry mob gathered, shouting "Hurrah for Jeff Davis!" and throwing brickbats. Presently someone shot an officer and the Union troops opened fire. At least twenty-eight civilians and two soldiers died in the ensuing melée, and dozens more were wounded.

Although provocative, Lyon's decision to disarm the militia was basically prudent. The prosecessionist militia had already received cannon and ammunition spirited to them from Louisiana; given time they might well have seized control of Saint Louis. Even so, his action and the ensuing riot fueled passions on both sides and promised further violence. To avert the possibility of more internal fighting, Missouri moderates arranged a meeting between Lyon and the prosecessionist governor. But after four hours of negotiation Lyon lost his temper. "Rather than concede to the State of Missouri for one instant the right to dictate to my Government in any matter . . . I would see you . . . and every man, woman, and child in the State, dead and buried. *This means war.*"

In the weeks that followed, Union forces managed to push the secessionist militia—without any major fighting—toward the southwestern part of Missouri. Lyon pursued with about 5,500 men and occupied the town of Springfield. But his forces dangled at the end of a tenuous supply line, he could receive no reinforcements, and soon the 8,000 secessionist militia (led by Major General Sterling Price) were joined by 5,000 Confederate troops under Major General Benjamin McCulloch. Lyon nevertheless refused to retreat and, learning that the Rebels would soon begin an offensive, decided to attack first. On August 10 he struck the enemy at Wilson's Creek, ten miles south of Springfield.

Lyon's attack was an incredible gamble that came amazingly close to success. The rebel troops were poorly trained and equipped, and Lyon managed to achieve surprise with a daring two-pronged attack. A confused, savage battle ensued along the banks of Wilson's Creek. Lyon's men managed to hold their own, despite odds of nearly three-to-one, until Lyon was fatally wounded. With his death the Union forces lost heart. Nearly out of ammunition anyway, they retreated. Eventually they fell back over one hundred miles to Rolla, a railhead town with links to Saint Louis.

Union losses in this battle were 1,300; Southern losses were about the same. The Confederates followed up their victory by marching into the Missouri River valley and capturing the important town of Lexington, Missouri, in mid-September. For a brief period, then, Price's militia controlled half the state. But Price soon discovered he lacked the manpower to hold such a vast region, and in October he withdrew again to the southwest corner of the state. In February 1862 a substantial Union army under Major General Samuel Curtis managed to eject Price from Missouri for good.

Then, in the Battle of Pea Ridge, Arkansas (March 6–8, 1862), Curtis stopped a major Confederate attempt to drive him back.

Almost despite itself, the Union had managed to hold on to Missouri. Its grip was tenuous and remained so. Throughout the war, Missouri was the scene of a continual and vicious guerrilla struggle, particularly in the proslavery Missouri River valley. Still, by early 1862 the Lincoln administration had achieved an important objective—it controlled the borderland.

First Bull Run

From a Union perspective, securing the borderland was a defensive goal. To do so might keep the rebellion within manageable limits, but it did little to defeat the Confederacy. For that the Union needed an offensive plan, and as the spring of 1861 progressed, the Lincoln administration pondered how best to proceed.

Its general-in-chief, the once magnificent but now aging Winfield Scott, proposed a very cautious strategy. Like many Northerners, including Lincoln, Scott believed that popular support for the Confederate regime was shallow; the Southern people, after all, had been until recently loyal citizens of the United States. An adroit approach might detach them from the Davis government and woo their allegiance back to the Union. But how to do this? Scott suggested a three-phase plan. First, blockade the Southern harbors, cutting them off from outside assistance. Second, send a strong column down the Mississippi River to hold that vital artery of commerce and further isolate the Confederate states. Third, wait. If the North did these things, Scott maintained, it "will thus cut off the luxuries to which the people are accustomed; and when they feel the pressure, not having been exasperated by attacks made on them within their respective States, the Union spirit will assert itself; those who are on the fence will descend on the Union side, and I will guarantee that in one year from this time all difficulties will be settled." If, on the other hand, Federal armies invaded the South at any point, "I will guarantee that at the end of a year you will be further from a settlement than you are now." The press, likening the strategy to the coilings of a giant constricting snake, soon dubbed Scott's proposal the "Anaconda Plan."

Some Cabinet members agreed with Scott, but most believed his plan would backfire. The longer the Confederate government functioned, the more legitimacy it would acquire in the minds of the Southern people. For this reason an immediate offensive against Richmond, the capital of that government, seemed imperative. Lincoln concurred with this second view and in late June gave orders that the Union forces assembling around Washington must advance against Richmond. The commander of these troops, Brigadier General Irvin McDowell, objected that his men were as yet too unseasoned for such an operation. Lincoln refused to budge. "You are green, it is true," he said. "But they [the Confederates] are green also. You are all green alike."

On July 16, 1861, McDowell left Washington with about 35,000 men. Twenty-five miles to the southwest lay a smaller Confederate army of

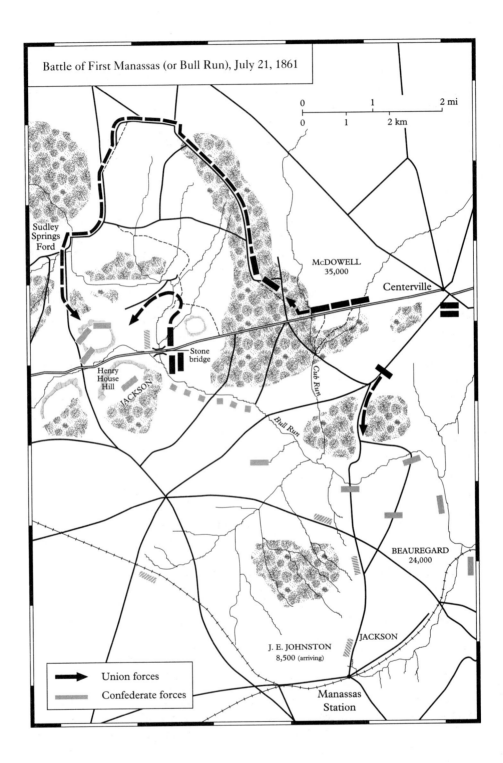

Battle of First Manassas (or Bull Run), July 21, 1861

Sudley Springs Ford

Stone bridge

Henry House Hill

JACKSON

Cub Run

Bull Run

McDOWELL
35,000

Centerville

BEAUREGARD
24,000

JACKSON

J. E. JOHNSTON
8,500 (arriving)

Manassas Station

0   1   2 mi
0   1   2 km

→ Union forces

▬ Confederate forces

25,000 men—led by General P. G. T. Beauregard, the victor of Fort Sumter. Beauregard had deployed his brigades along a lengthy stretch of a bramble-choked stream called Bull Run. From this position Beauregard's army held the railroad town of Manassas Junction and blocked the direct overland approach to Richmond.

McDowell outnumbered Beauregard by a considerable margin, and if the Confederates at Manassas had fought unaided he might have won a considerable victory. But fifty miles to the west, 13,000 Rebels under General Joseph E. Johnston guarded the lower Shenandoah Valley. Opposing them was a somewhat larger Union force under an elderly militia general named Robert Patterson. Patterson's mission was to prevent Johnston from reinforcing Beauregard once McDowell advanced; however, he botched the assignment. Leaving a thin screen of cavalry to deceive Patterson, Johnston loaded most of his troops on railcars and sent them rolling down the Manassas Gap Railroad. They reached the Bull Run position on the afternoon of July 21, just as McDowell was pressing home a skillfully prepared attack upon Beauregard's beleaguered men. These reinforcements (coupled with a tenacious defense by Confederate Brigadier General Thomas J. Jackson, who earned the nickname "Stonewall" for his role in the battle) turned the tide against the Federals. Then, just as McDowell had feared, the inexperience of the Union troops transformed a reversal into a rout. The Northerners streamed back toward Washington in a disheveled, uncontrollable mass. It might just as easily have happened to the equally inexperienced Confederates. But it did not, and the Battle of Bull Run became a symbol of Southern prowess and Northern humiliation.

The Union lost about 625 killed in this first major engagement, along with 950 wounded and over 1,200 captured; Confederate casualties numbered 400 killed and about 1,600 wounded. By itself, the battle decided nothing. But in the South it created a sense of dangerous overconfidence, while Northerners regarded it as a stinging summons to greater efforts. From a purely military standpoint its most interesting aspect was the Confederates' use of the railroad to reinforce the threatened Bull Run sector. Without the railroad, Johnston's troops would have reached the battlefield too exhausted for action—if indeed they would have arrived at all.

Cracking the Confederate Frontier

Railroads played a significant role in the struggle for the borderland. The Union thrust into western Virginia was dictated, to a considerable degree, by the need to control the Baltimore & Ohio Railroad, one of the main east-west trunk lines. The Union offensive in Missouri also followed the railroad as far as possible. Meanwhile, along the coast and in the trans-Appalachian west, the Union began to exploit the nineteenth century's other great agent of mechanized power: the steamship. In the months that followed the Bull Run defeat, the Union's edge in sea and riverine power helped it recover from this initial setback. Federal warships began the long, slow process of strangling the South's commerce by blockading its ports, and using Union troops to secure a number of enclaves along the Confederate coast. And in the Mississippi River valley, Union gunboats and transports played a major role in the North's first decisive victories during the winter of 1862.

The Coast, 1861–1862

The seceded states had nearly 3,000 miles of coastline. In part this formed a Confederate asset, because it offered nearly eighty points where Southern blockade runners could find safe harbor. But the long coastline was also a major liability, because it gave Union forces wide opportunity to exploit the North's command of the sea. Defending the long, vulnerable sea frontier diverted many thousands of Confederate troops from duty with the field armies. Even so, Union troops generally had little trouble seizing whatever coastal point they chose. From a Southern perspective, the situation was depressingly like that of the colonists during the American Revolution. The revolutionary general Charles Lee once complained that he felt "like a dog in a dancing school" when confronted by superior British sea mobility. A number of Confederate generals grew familiar with the same sensation.

The first Union beachheads were established primarily as coaling

Union landing at Hatteras Inlet, August 1861. The Union had a formidable edge over the Confederacy in sea power, and troops transported by the U.S. Navy established numerous enclaves along the Southern coast during the course of the Civil War. The enclaves supported the Union blockade and provided springboards for advances inland.

stations for blockaders. In August 1861 a Northern detachment occupied Hatteras Inlet, North Carolina; three months later a larger force seized the magnificent harbor at Port Royal, South Carolina. By March 1862 additional troops had occupied much of eastern North Carolina. Once established, these enclaves provided bases from which Union troops could raid inland. Perhaps as importantly, they acted like magnets for hundreds of slaves who escaped their masters and took refuge within Union lines.

Many of these initial amphibious operations pitted Union warships against the casemated forts that had formed America's principal defensive network since the republic's early years. Conventional wisdom held that in a slugging match between ships and forts, the forts would inevitably prevail, but events challenged this old notion. Armed with the new Columbiad and Dahlgren shell-firing guns, Union warships routinely reduced forts within a few hours. Steam power also made it possible for warships to navigate with greater precision in shallow coastal waters, so that they could perform feats that might have proved fatal for older sailing craft.

The greatest single victory for Union sea power occurred in April 1862, when a Federal fleet engaged the two forts that guarded the Mississippi River below New Orleans. Assisted by a flotilla of mortar boats that rained heavy shells into the forts, the fleet—led by Flag Officer David G. Farragut—managed to steam past the forts and on to nearly defenseless New Orleans. On April 25, Union troops hoisted the Stars and Stripes above the port's customs house. The Confederacy's largest city was gone. Just as bad, Union warships now had access to a long stretch of the lower Mississippi River.

The Emergence of Grant

As the Federal navy prepared to attack New Orleans, a joint force of Northern ground troops and gunboats penetrated the Confederacy's long, vulnerable frontier along the Tennessee-Kentucky border. In the fall of 1861 the rebel general Albert Sidney Johnston—widely considered the South's ablest commander—had constructed a defensive cordon that ran from Columbus, Kentucky, on the Mississippi River to Cumberland Gap in the Appalachian Mountains. Just south of the Tennessee-Kentucky border his troops had also built two major works—Forts Henry and Donelson—to bar Federal navigation on the Tennessee and Cumberland rivers, respectively.

But Johnston had only 43,000 men to hold this 300-mile line. The Federals confronted Johnston with more than twice that many troops, but three factors combined to reduce this numerical edge. First, a significant portion of Union strength had to protect lines of communication once Federal offensive operations began. Second, their massive logistical needs compelled Union armies to move only where railroad or river transportation was available. That, in turn, limited the Federals to just four avenues of approach to the south: down the Mississippi River against Columbus; up the Tennessee River to Fort Henry; up the Cumberland River to Fort Donelson; or along the Louisville & Nashville Railroad to Bowling Green in

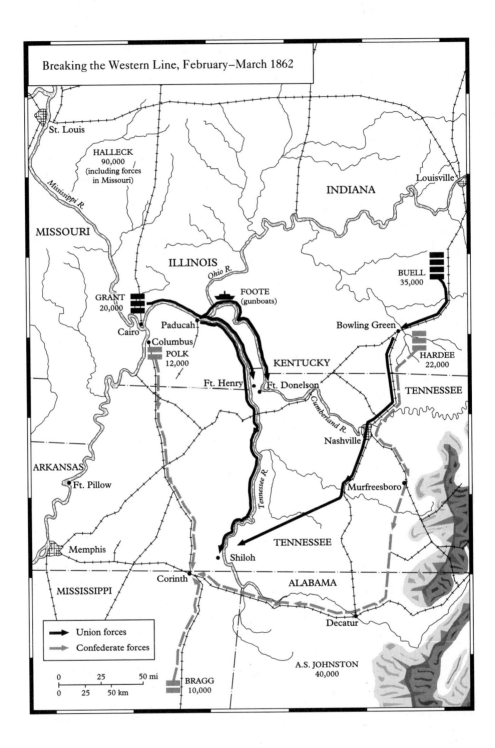

Breaking the Western Line, February–March 1862

south-central Kentucky. Johnston could read a map as well as anyone and had placed most of his forces to block these approaches.

The greatest difficulty affecting the Union high command, however, was of its own making. Whereas Johnston enjoyed complete authority within his theater of operations, the Lincoln administration had divided the same region into two parts: the Department of Missouri, commanded by Major General Henry W. Halleck; and the Department of the Ohio, led by Major General Don Carlos Buell. Their operations could be coordinated only by a third party, Major General George B. McClellan in faraway Washington. Complicating this awkward arrangement were the personalities of the three generals themselves. All were cautious by nature, all displayed great sensitivity about their own administrative domains, and all believed that if the enemy possessed interior lines—an advantage the Confederates actually did possess at the moment—then any attacking force must labor at a forbidding disadvantage. Consequently, this timid, touchy triumvirate dawdled over adopting a plan to crack Johnston's line.

Ultimately this delay was overcome less by any decision on the part of these generals than by the initiative of Brigadier General Ulysses S. Grant, a key Halleck subordinate. The chain of events began early in January 1862, when Grant received orders to take a small force up the Tennessee River and make a diversionary demonstration against Fort Henry. He did so, discovered the fort was much less formidable than previously believed, and urged Halleck to let him attack the fort. As soon as he received Halleck's approval, Grant piled about 15,000 troops aboard transports and

The South's many navigable rivers gave Northern forces excellent access to the Confederate interior, and Union gunboats often cooperated effectively with Union land forces. Sometimes they even accomplished important results on their own, as in their unassisted capture of Fort Henry, Tennessee, in February 1862.

headed up the Tennessee River. A flotilla of gunboats, commanded by Flag Officer Andrew H. Foote, steamed along in support of the expedition. On February 6, Grant landed a few miles below Fort Henry while Foote's gunboats steamed upriver to shell the place. To everyone's surprise, the fort surrendered almost at once. Winter rains had raised the Tennessee to flood stage; most of the fort was under six feet of water. The garrison commander had sent most of his 2,500 men to Fort Donelson, twelve miles east, leaving only a handful of artillerists to confront Foote's naval squadron. After a brief bombardment the Confederates ran up the white flag. The boat crew sent to receive the surrender sailed right through the rebel sally port, and the navy, not Grant, captured Fort Henry.

Things then happened very quickly. With no further fortifications blocking navigation of the Tennessee, Foote's gunboats raided upstream as far south as Muscle Shoals, Alabama. Grant notified Halleck that he planned to attack Fort Donelson at once. Johnston, meanwhile, took the defeat at Fort Henry as a signal that his defensive cordon could not hold much longer. He withdrew part of the garrison at Columbus, abandoned Bowling Green, and sent substantial reinforcements to Fort Donelson.

Reinforcing the fort proved a mistake. On February 13, Grant's army—now increased to about 23,000—invested Donelson. The following day Foote's gunboats attacked and tried to repeat their success at Fort Henry. This time a Confederate fort managed to hold its own. Seriously damaged, the Union flotilla had to retire. Even so, the generals inside Fort Donelson believed Grant would soon surround the place. They elected to break out to the south. The attempt succeeded. But then, incredibly, they ordered everyone to return to the Donelson trenches. After a bizarre council of war in which the two senior commanders abdicated their responsibilities and escaped the fort, the number-three man, Brigadier General Simon Bolivar Buckner, sent a flag of truce to Grant and requested terms of surrender.

Grant's response made him an instantaneous celebrity in the North. "No terms except unconditional and immediate surrender can be accepted. I propose to move immediately upon your works." The terse ultimatum miffed Buckner, who thought it ungenerous, but he had little choice save to accept. The next day approximately 12,500 Confederates lay down their arms. It was the first major Union victory of the war.

With Fort Donelson gone, Federal gunboats could now range up the Cumberland River as well. Nashville, Tennessee's capital city and an important supply center, was abandoned by the Confederates without a fight. Johnston's forces were now in full retreat. Grant's army moved up the Tennessee River to within a few miles of the Mississippi state line. Buell's command, meanwhile, occupied Nashville and advanced cautiously toward a junction with Grant.

Grant's army took up position at a stopping point for Tennessee River steamboats known as Pittsburg Landing. Pittsburg Landing possessed only two significant attributes: it had enough level ground nearby to permit an encampment for 40,000 men; and it was only about twenty miles from the little town of Corinth, Mississippi.

Because of two key railroads intersecting there, Corinth formed the main Federal objective point in the west. North and south ran the Mobile and Ohio line. East and west ran the Memphis and Charleston Railroad—a major trunk line and, in effect, the Confederacy's backbone. Union military and political leaders widely believed that if the Union could occupy two points in the South the rebellion would collapse. One of them was Richmond. Corinth was the other.

General Albert Sidney Johnston also concentrated the Confederate forces that had recently abandoned the Kentucky-Tennessee line in the little Mississippi rail town. In addition, President Jefferson Davis saw to it that Johnston got reinforcements from all over the South, so that by the end of March about 40,000 troops had collected around Corinth. On April 3, Johnston placed the entire force on the road to Pittsburg Landing.

Johnston understood that in numerical terms his army was barely equivalent to Grant's. He knew as well that most of his troops had never been in combat and that many of them were armed only with shotguns and old flintlock muskets. But he also recognized that he had only one chance to redress Confederate fortunes in the west. If he could hit Grant's army at once he might achieve surprise, press it back against the Tennesssee River, and destroy it. If he waited more than a few days, Buell's troops would join those of Grant, the numerical odds would become forbidding, and there would be little choice but to concede western and middle Tennessee to the Federals for good.

The roads were bad and the troops unseasoned. It required two full days to negotiate the twenty miles from Corinth to the Union encampment, and along the way the raw Southern troops made so much noise it seemed impossible the Federals could remain unaware of the impending attack. P. G. T. Beauregard, the hero of Manassas and now Johnston's second-in-command, urged that the offensive be abandoned. Johnston would have none of it. "I would fight them if they were a million," he reportedly said, and on the evening of April 5 he deployed his troops for battle.

Shiloh

The terrain around Pittsburg Landing was typical of many Civil War battlefields. The ground was heavily wooded, cut by ravines, and choked with undergrowth. Two sluggish little creeks enveloped the Union encampment and flowed indolently into the Tennessee River. The roads in the area— hardly more than forest tracks—connected a few widely separated farm lots. Bordering the main road from the landing to Corinth was a little wooden church known as Shiloh Meeting House.

Amazingly the Federals had almost no inkling of the impending Confederate attack. A few Union officers suspected something was afoot, but when they approached the senior general in the area—a grizzled redhead named William Tecumseh Sherman—their fears were brusquely dismissed. Convinced the Confederates remained demoralized after their recent defeats, Sherman refused to entertain even the idea that they might launch a counterstroke. "Take your damn regiment back to Ohio," he snarled at one

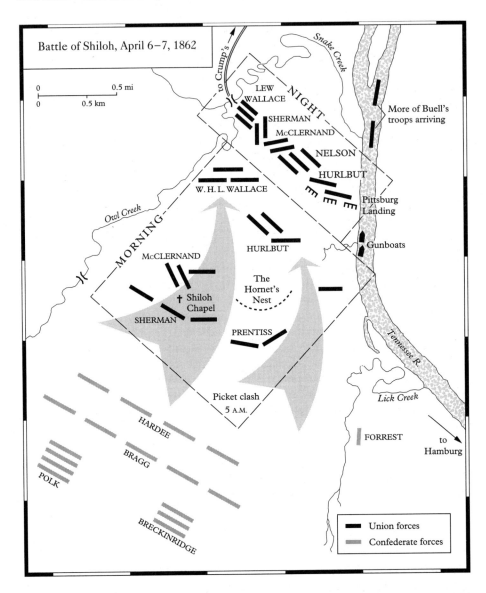

Battle of Shiloh, April 6–7, 1862

nervous colonel. "There is no enemy nearer than Corinth." Grant shared this view of things, and although he visited the encampment on April 5 he felt assured enough to retain his headquarters at Savannah, a town some ten miles downstream. Neither Grant nor Sherman gave orders for the troops to entrench.

Despite some security precautions the Federals were taken largely by surprise on the morning of Sunday, April 6, when Johnston's army came boiling out of the woods. They came in waves, with each of the four Confederate corps piling in one behind the other. Although this unorthodox formation helped the attack get off to a quicker start—it would have required additional hours to deploy the corps in conventional fashion—it soon created severe problems of command and control. The rebel troops crashed through the Federal encampments shortly after dawn, drove the terrified Unionists back toward Pittsburg Landing, and tried to press home their attack. But units from the various corps soon became intermingled, so that by midday the Confederate brigade and division commanders increasingly found themselves trying to lead nothing more than huge armed mobs. Troops who had never seen each other, much less trained together, were forced to carry out Johnston's demanding all-or-nothing offensive.

The Federals were, in some cases, equally disorganized. Thousands—possibly as many as one-fourth of Grant's army—simply ran for the shelter of the steep bluffs that rose from Pittsburg Landing. The rest stayed with their divisions and fought with determination, only to discover time and again that Confederate troops had lapped around their flanks, forcing them to retreat.

Grant reached the battle around 8:30 A.M. The scene that confronted him was ghastly. The thousands of men who had fled the battle now crowded the bluffs at Pittsburg Landing. Beyond them the woodlands around Shiloh Meeting House shook with the concussion of rifle fire and the screams of men. Grant quickly ordered more ammunition brought up and detailed two regiments to round up stragglers. For the rest of the day he rode back and forth along the battle line, pausing now and then to confer with his division commanders. He could see that the battle had degenerated into a huge slugging match, devoid of tactical finesse. For the Federals the important thing seemed just to hold on long enough for reinforcements to arrive.

Near the Union center, Brigadier General Benjamin M. Prentiss's division withdrew to the cover of a narrow road running parallel to the Confederate front. Grant gave Prentiss an emphatic order to hold the position at all costs. The order was obeyed. Prentiss's men drowned every attempt to dislodge them in a hail of gunfire. Before long, with bitter respect, Southerners attacking the position began calling it the "Hornet's Nest."

Meanwhile the remaining Union forces withdrew slowly, grudgingly, against furious but diminishing thrusts by the rebel army. Exactly as instructed, Prentiss held on grimly to the Hornet's Nest. Only at 5:30 P.M., with the position entirely surrounded, did he reluctantly surrender his men. His stand made it possible for Grant's chief artillerist to plant fifty cannon a quarter-mile from the landing and end the threat of the Confederates pushing on to the river. Sundown brought an end to the day's fighting. During the night, while rainstorms lashed the battlefield and surgeons worked feverishly in improvised hospitals, Wallace's and Buell's forces finally arrived. Numbering about 28,000 men, they more than offset Union losses during the day.

Despite the arrival of reinforcements, most of Grant's officers were extremely discouraged. Many of them, including Sherman, believed retreat might be the best course. During the day, Sherman had fought his division with coolness and determination, but he still believed the army had lost this battle and late that night he sought out Grant to tell him so. He found his commander standing beneath a tree in a downpour, rain dripping from his hat, a cigar smoldering between his teeth. Something in Grant's demeanor made Sherman decide not to discuss retreat. Instead he said simply, "Well,

When Ulysses S. Grant won the Union's first major victory at Fort Donelson in February 1862, his capture of 12,000 Confederates made him a hero in the North. But two months later, criticism of his conduct at Shiloh discouraged him so much that he briefly considered resigning.

Grant, we've had the devil's own day, haven't we?" "Yes," Grant agreed, then added: "Lick 'em in the morning, though." Ultimately his stubborn strength made the difference between victory and defeat at Shiloh.

The following day events went as Grant predicted—the Federals "licked" the Confederates. The Southerners, like their Northern counterparts, were utterly exhausted by Sunday's battle. They had gotten badly disorganized and suffered huge numbers of stragglers. They had even lost their commanding general: the previous afternoon a bullet had clipped one of Sidney Johnston's arteries, causing him to bleed to death within minutes. Worst of all, the Confederates had no fresh units to feed into the struggle. Although they fought grimly throughout Monday, April 7, the strongly reinforced Union army ground them down. At sunset, the Rebels began a sullen retreat to Corinth.

The Battle of Shiloh horrified both North and South. In two days' fighting the Confederate army lost 10,699 men killed, wounded, or missing; Union casualties totaled 13,047. The North American continent had never endured anything like it. Shiloh's cost in human lives far exceeded that of any engagement in previous American experience. Losses were five times those of Bull Run. The battle virtually doubled the year-old war's casualty figures. Northerners who considered this shattering toll found it impossible to regard the battle as a Union victory. It seemed more like an unmitigated disaster, and many who had praised Grant a few weeks earlier now clamored for his removal.

Yet Shiloh *was* a Union victory, and a big one, for it confirmed the previous Federal successes at Forts Henry and Donelson. The Confederacy had lost much of western and middle Tennessee, and the Union's victory at Shiloh ensured that the Rebels would not regain this region. Two additional victories soon consolidated the Union's success. On April 7 a force of 30,000 men under Brigadier General John Pope captured Island No. 10, a

Confederate fortress blocking navigation of the Mississippi River near the Kentucky-Tennessee line. And on June 5 a Union flotilla seized Memphis after a brief but savage naval battle.

★   ★   ★   ★

The first year of the Civil War saw the conflict assume very wide dimensions that readily eclipsed any previous war on American soil. Both North and South had created and fielded large armies, led by a combination of professional and amateur officers and manned by enthusiastic though as yet unseasoned volunteers. Both sides were performing at a level much better than American forces during the War of 1812, testimony to the leadership exerted at the top by West Point graduates. The Union side in particular had managed some very creditable feats of army-navy cooperation.

By the end of spring 1862, Federal and Confederate armies had also fought a number of battles that demonstrated that the war would be much bloodier than previous American struggles. Part of this heightened lethality owed to the impact of the rifled musket, but most of it was due to the increased size of the rival armies and the earnestness with which both sides fought. The casualty figures were not exceptional by European standards— Shiloh was no worse than some of the battles fought by Frederick the Great. They seemed worse, perhaps, because the men who were killed and wounded were much more representative of their parent societies than professional European forces were of theirs.

The Northern cause had made excellent progress during the war's first year. Despite a serious early reverse at Bull Run, Union troops had managed to retain control of the crucial border states, to accquire a number of enclaves along the Southern coastline, and to impose a naval blockade of the Confederacy. Most promisingly, they had also broken the Confederate defensive cordon in the western theater. Taken together, these victories suggested that it might well be possible to destroy the rebellion and restore the Union without having to address the politically explosive slavery issue or to destroy large amounts of Southern property.

All eyes now turned to McClellan's great campaign against Richmond. The first six months of 1862 had brought a string of victories: Forts Henry and Donelson, the seizure of the North Carolina coast, the battles of Pea Ridge and Shiloh, the capture of New Orleans, Island No. 10, and Memphis. The Confederacy had been bludgeoned along its entire frontier. Everyone now expected the Army of the Potomac to deliver the death blow.

SUGGESTED READINGS

Catton, Bruce. *The Coming Fury*. (Garden City, N.Y.: Doubleday, 1961).

———. *Terrible Swift Sword*. (Garden City, N.Y.: Doubleday, 1964).

Connelly, Thomas L. *Army of the Heartland: The Army of Tennessee, 1861–1862* (Baton Rouge: Louisiana State University Press, 1967).

Connelly, Thomas L., and Archer Jones. *The Politics of Command: Factions and Ideas in Confederate Strategy* (Baton Rouge: Louisiana State University Press, 1973).

Cooling, Benjamin F. *Forts Henry and Donelson: The Key to the Confederate Heartland* (Knoxville: University of Tennessee Press, 1987).

Davis, William C. *Battle at Bull Run* (Garden City, N.Y.: Doubleday, 1977).

Hattaway, Herman, and Archer Jones. *How the North Won: A Military History of the Civil War* (Urbana: University of Illinois Press, 1983).

Linderman, Gerald F. *Embattled Courage: The Experience of Combat in the American Civil War* (New York: Free Press, 1987).

McDonough, James Lee. *Shiloh: In Hell Before Night* (Knoxville: University of Tennessee Press, 1977).

McPherson, James M. *Battle Cry of Freedom: The Civil War Era* (New York: Oxford University Press, 1988).

Nevins, Allan, *The War for the Union,* 4 vols. (New York: Charles Scribner's Sons, 1959–1971).

Potter, David M. *The Impending Crisis, 1848–1861* (New York: Harper, 1976).

Williams, Kenneth P. *Lincoln Finds a General,* 5 vols. (New York: Macmillan, 1949–1956).

Williams, T. Harry. *Lincoln and His Generals* (New York: Alfred A. Knopf, 1952).

Woodworth, Steven E. *Jefferson Davis and His Generals: The Failure of Confederate Command in the West* (Lawrence: University Press of Kansas, 1990).

3

THE CIVIL WAR, 1862:
ENDING THE LIMITED WAR

"A Single Grand Campaign"
The Failure of Limited War
Confederate Counterstrokes
Autumn Stalemate

By early June 1862 the war seemed all but over. The border states, including western Virginia, were solidly in Union hands. Federal units controlled the lower Mississippi River from the delta to New Orleans and also held the middle reaches of the river as far south as Memphis. Halleck's armies had captured western Tennessee, controlled much of middle Tennessee, and pressed into northern Alabama. Most importantly they had seized the strategic railroad junction at Corinth, Mississippi. This last victory had been virtually bloodless. Halleck's huge force—numbering well over 100,000 men—had crept toward the rail town barely a mile per day. At night it dug extensive entrenchments; Halleck wanted no repetition of the damaging surprise attack at Shiloh. By the end of May, Beauregard, who now commanded Sidney Johnston's army, prudently abandoned Corinth and slipped away to Tupelo, some eighty miles south. Some Northerners regretted the Confederate escape but most simply smiled at this latest Yankee triumph.

Then, abruptly, the Union dream of victory was shattered. McClellan's great offensive against Richmond collapsed. Not only did the rebel capital elude capture, but the Confederate army in the east then began a series of aggressive counterstrokes that carried the war, in a matter of weeks, from the shores of the James River to the banks of the Potomac. In the western theater other Confederate armies carried out similar offensives of their own. With sickening swiftness, many in the North realized that the war would not be short or easy and that its conduct had to change. Until then the Lincoln administration had waged a limited war. Its armies had aimed their blows exclusively against rebel military units and had tried, as far as possible, to preserve the constitutional rights of Southern civilians—including the right to hold slaves. Now many in the North clamored that this "kid glove" warfare, as it was derisively called, must end. The Lincoln administration agreed. The reversals of summer 1862 led directly to the collapse of limited war and the advent of new, more severe measures against the South.

Another development that marked this period was the deployment of the *corps d'armée,* a military organization that had not existed at all in previous American wars. Although nominally begun during the early months of 1862—McClellan adopted the corps system in March 1862 and then Sidney Johnston used a similar arrangement at Shiloh—the corps organization was at first mainly an administrative expedient. Not until midsummer did the corps emerge as an operational unit. From then on, the Union and Confederate armies utilized the corps system not only to control large masses of men more effectively but also to maneuver against one another's flank and rear and, when necessary, to fight independently. Civil War armies began to march and fight in the classic Napoleonic style.

"A Single Grand Campaign"

The greatest hope for an early Union victory reposed in the person of Major General George B. McClellan. Just thirty-four years old when the war broke out, McClellan had quickly risen to high command. Although he had left the army in 1856 to become a railroad executive, his West Point training brought him at once to the attention of Ohio's governor, who placed him in charge of the state's volunteer forces. In the early summer of 1861 he had won a series of minor victories in western Virginia that brought him considerable laurels. Newspapers began calling him "the Napoleon of the present war." When, after the debacle at Bull Run, Lincoln looked about for a commander to replace McDowell, he speedily settled on McClellan.

Arriving in Washington on July 27, McClellan was appalled by the confused condition of McDowell's battered troops. But he quickly rebuilt the force around Washington, which he soon dubbed the Army of the Potomac. In early August, at Lincoln's request, he also sent the president a memorandum detailing his conceptions for winning the war. McClellan wanted most Union strength concentrated for a single, overwhelming thrust against Richmond. To achieve this objective the young general sought to create a juggernaut of 273,000 men and 600 cannon. McClellan's rationale for his plan was largely political. Like many Northerners, he believed the common people of the South were lukewarm in their support for the Confederate government. In McClellan's view, only a display of overwhelming military force, coupled with a lenient policy toward Southern civilians, could create the conditions for a restoration of the Union. Implicit in his plan was the conviction that a lengthy struggle would embitter both North and South and make reunion more difficult.

Called the "Young Napoleon" by an admiring public, George B. McClellan was a talented organizer, a charismatic leader, and a good strategic planner, but he was ultimately hamstrung by frictions with the Lincoln administration and an overcaution verging on timidity.

The vigorous style of McClellan's memorandum promised action, but its substance suggested delay. The young commander did not want to go off half-cocked. He needed time to amass and train the huge army he contemplated, and indeed it is difficult to see how McClellan could have begun this great offensive much before the spring of 1862. Unfortunately, from the outset he never made this clear to either the public or his political superiors. Instead he let them believe that he might commence major offensive actions during the autumn of 1861, and when no sign of this offensive materialized, his near-unanimous bipartisan support began to fade. Democrats and conservative Republicans continued to back McClellan, but the radical wing of the Republican party turned sharply against him.

It did not help that McClellan detested Lincoln, whom he termed "the original Gorilla." Lincoln nevertheless displayed amazing patience with McClellan and in November 1861 even appointed him general-in-chief. But as the months slid by without action, Lincoln's confidence in McClellan declined. Mutual distrust between the president and his chief commander characterized every phase of the great Richmond offensive when it finally began.

Genesis of the Peninsula Campaign

After the Bull Run defeat the strategic situation in Virginia looked like this. McClellan's army held the Union capital and a long stretch of the Potomac River both north and south of the city. The Confederate army, under General Joseph E. Johnston, was concentrated at Centreville, just up the road from the old Bull Run battlefield. The Rebels had also erected batteries that interdicted passage of the lower Potomac River and, in effect, placed Washington under a partial blockade.

By September, McClellan had gathered over 100,000 troops into his Army of the Potomac. Johnston, by contrast, had barely 40,000. Had McClellan been so disposed he might well have advanced directly against the Confederates, but instead he did nothing. McClellan defended his inaction by claiming that Johnston had 150,000 troops, the estimate given to him by Allan Pinkerton, his chief of intelligence. If Johnston really did have 150,000 men, of course, an overland offensive stood little chance of success. Thus McClellan always looked for alternatives. By December he had settled on a scheme to convey most of the Army of the Potomac by sea to Urbanna, a small town on the Rappahannock River about fifty miles northeast of Richmond. This would cut in half the overland distance the army must cover; better yet, it would render the Confederate lines at Centreville untenable, force Johnston's army into precipitate retreat, and possibly create advantageous conditions for a Union attack.

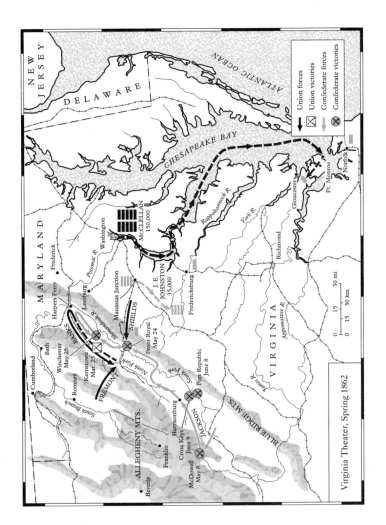

Virginia Theater, Spring 1862

Unfortunately for McClellan, a Confederate redeployment soon rendered his original plan all but impossible. Johnston had long regarded his Centreville position as too exposed. On March 8–9, 1862, the rebel army therefore fell back to a new position behind the Rappahannock in central Virginia. With Johnston's army now much closer to Urbanna and Richmond, the strategic rationale for the Urbanna scheme largely disappeared. Accordingly, McClellan switched to an alternate plan. The Army of the Potomac would still move against Richmond by sea, but instead of landing at Urbanna it would disembark at Fort Monroe. This Union-held outpost lay at the tip of a long peninsula formed by the York and James rivers. It was not so close to Richmond as Urbanna—seventy-five miles as opposed to fifty—and the route to the Confederate capital was blocked by a small force stationed at Yorktown, but it still seemed preferable to an overland advance.

Before beginning the great campaign, McClellan took his army on a brief shakedown march to the abandoned Confederate position at Centreville. This served only to exacerbate his already considerable political difficulties, for it soon became obvious that the lines could not possibly have held 150,000 men. Lincoln's doubts about McClellan increased, and on March 12 the president removed him as general-in-chief. Lincoln explained the change by saying that once McClellan took the field he would be fully occupied with command of the Army of the Potomac. The young commander, however, regarded it as an implied rebuke, as it almost certainly was. McClellan began his great campaign under a cloud.

From Yorktown to Seven Pines

The transfer of McClellan's army to Fort Monroe began on March 17. Since the U.S. government possessed nowhere near enough vessels for so great a task, it chartered every available steamer from Maryland to Maine: 113 in all, as well as an additional 276 smaller vessels. Within three weeks 121,500 men, 14,492 animals, 1,224 wagons, and over 200 cannon had reached the tip of the Virginia peninsula. It was—as one astonished British observer remarked—"the stride of a giant" and it showed the extent of the North's advantage in sea power.

The advance inland began on April 4. But just twenty-four hours later it ceased abruptly when Union troops encountered a belt of Confederate fortifications extending across the peninsula from Yorktown to the James River. The existence of this line, while not altogether unexpected, convinced McClellan that a formal siege would be necessary for its reduction. His decision further strained his already poor relationship with the Lincoln administration. Relations became even worse when the administration discovered that McClellan had left nowhere near enough troops to defend Washington during the Army of the Potomac's absence. As a result it withheld McClellan's I Corps—some 40,000 men—and retained it in northern Virginia.

McClellan, furious, now found that he must "crush the rebellion at a single blow" with a significantly reduced force. Nevertheless, although he refused to believe it, he handily outnumbered the Confederates facing him, even after most of Johnston's army abandoned the Rappahannock line and came down to Yorktown. Well aware of his numerical disadvantage, Johnston remarked, "Nobody but McClellan would have hesitated to attack."

For nearly a month, Federal engineers and artillerists sweated to emplace the mammoth siege guns that would blast the Yorktown defenders into oblivion. Johnston, however, did not wait to be blasted. On May 1 he notified Richmond authorities that the Yorktown position was untenable, that he intended to withdraw, and that all possible reinforcements should be concentrated near the Confederate capital. Two nights later his army left Yorktown.

The retreat had severe strategic costs. It opened the York and James rivers to Federal gunboats, led to the abandonment of Norfolk and its navy yard, and forced the scuttling of the daunting Confederate ironclad warship *Virginia*. For a brief time Confederate authorities even contemplated the evacuation of Richmond, but Jefferson Davis's military advisor, General Robert E. Lee, made a passionate plea for the capital's continued defense.

Fortunately for the South, at that point Confederate defenses began to stiffen. On May 15 several artillery batteries at Drewry's Bluff, below Richmond, rebuffed the Federal navy's lunge up the James River. In the Shenandoah Valley, troops under Major General Thomas J. "Stonewall" Jackson, a dour ex-professor of the Virginia Military Institute, won a series of astonishing small victories over much larger Union forces. And although by the end of May McClellan's massive army had come to within seven miles of Richmond, it advanced gingerly. Moreover, it was clear that McClellan, instead of launching an immediate attack, planned to conduct a siege of Richmond.

McClellan had placed his main supply base at White House Landing on the Pamunkey River. A short rail line from Richmond had its terminus there, which offered a reliable way to transport his heavy siege guns to the front. But his choice of base meant that his army had to straddle the Chickahominy River northeast of Richmond. Heavy spring rains rendered the stream almost impassable, thus dividing the Army of the Potomac. On May 31, Johnston took advantage of this and tried to crush the southern wing of McClellan's army in the Battle of Seven Pines. But nothing went right. Johnston's plans were vague and his management of the battle was terrible. The Confederates lost 6,000 troops; the Union, about 5,000. The most important result of the two-day battle was that on June 1 Johnston was severely wounded. To succeed him, Davis appointed Robert E. Lee.

In June 1862, Lee was still comparatively unknown in the South, and what Southerners did know of him they did not like. Although a well-respected figure in the prewar U.S. Army and one of the highest ranking officers to side with the Confederacy, Lee's wartime career to date had been disappointing. In the autumn of 1861 he had conducted a brief, ineffectual campaign in the western Virginia mountains that earned him the derisive nickname "Granny" Lee. In March 1862, President Davis had appointed him his military advisor, a seemingly imposing assignment but one with little formal authority. Small wonder that many Southerners were dismayed to find Lee in charge of Richmond's defense.

Jackson in the Valley

What few knew, however, was that Lee had pronounced ideas about aggressive action. Indeed he had already tried them out. His partner in this venture was "Stonewall" Jackson. The arena in which they tried out their offensive scheme was the Shenandoah Valley. One of the most productive agricultural regions in North America, the Valley also had qualities that arrested the strategist's eye. Its farms produced much of the Confederacy's grain and many of its horses. The Baltimore & Ohio Railroad ran across its northern reaches; thus any Confederate force in full control of the valley also controlled the Union's single most important east-west communications link. And the sheltering mountains on either side made the Valley a natural avenue of invasion into Maryland and Pennsylvania. For these reasons both Federals and Confederates sought to possess the region.

In the fall of 1861 the defense of the Valley became Jackson's responsibility. With only 4,500 men under his command, Jackson's position was precarious from the outset, and in early March 1862, some 38,000 Federals under Major General Nathaniel Banks entered the northern part of the Valley and drove him away from Winchester, the region's largest town. After a short pursuit, Banks left a single division of 9,000 men at Winchester and withdrew the rest back toward Washington. On March 23, hoping to defeat the lone division at Winchester, Jackson attacked.

He failed, but the bold Confederate attack convinced his opponent that Jackson had either received reinforcements or expected them shortly. As a result, Banks returned to the Valley with a second division of 9,000 men. Then Lincoln detached a 10,000-man division from the Army of the Potomac and ordered it to join Major General John C. Frémont's forces in western Virginia, on the theory that if Jackson were strong enough to attack at Winchester he might threaten Frémont as well. Nor was this all. The fact that Banks was no longer available to cover Washington, D.C., during McClellan's germinating peninsula campaign helped spur Lincoln to withdraw McDowell's 40,000-man corps from McClellan's control (as mentioned earlier) and retain it in northern Virginia. Jackson's battlefield defeat thus turned into strategic success; it tied up the movements of nearly 60,000 Federal troops.

It also set the stage for Lee's first major attempt at an offensive-defensive strategy. By mid-April the Confederates in Virginia faced four main threats, of which McClellan was merely the largest. Banks's corps was advancing and had reached Harrisonburg in the central Valley; McDowell's corps in northern Virginia could march south at any time. Frémont's forces in western Virginia also seemed active, and McClellan of course menaced Richmond itself. In every instance the Federals far outnumbered the rebel forces opposing them. A passive defense could never hope to resist so many pressures.

Lee believed the only solution was to combine against one of the Northern forces, eliminate it, and thus dislocate the remaining Union forces. On April 21 he wrote to Jackson suggesting that Jackson should link up with a division led by Major General Richard S. Ewell. He would then hurl his augmented force against Banks's isolated corps. Jackson, however, replied that even with Ewell's help, he would still need 5,000 more troops to attack with any chance of success. When Lee could not furnish the extra 5,000, Jackson proposed a modified plan. Instead of striking Banks, he would unite with 2,800 troops under Confederate Major General Edward Johnson and hit Frémont's advance guard. Then, using both Ewell and Johnson, he would attack Banks. Lee approved the plan and on May 8, Jackson defeated Frémont at the Battle of McDowell, Virginia.

Jackson's victory inaugurated one of the classic campaigns of military history. Reinforced to about 10,000 men after the Battle of McDowell, Jackson united with Ewell—thereby adding another 7,000 troops to his command—and lunged northward toward Banks. Thoroughly misleading the Union commander, Jackson appeared in front of Banks, then suddenly swung around the Union flank, using cavalry to screen his movement. On May 23 he captured a small Union garrison at Front Royal; Banks now frantically withdrew down the Valley before Jackson could cut off his retreat. At

When a series of major defeats shook the Confederacy in early 1862, the exploits of Major General Thomas J. "Stonewall" Jackson helped bolster Southern morale. His campaign in the Shenandoah Valley is still considered a military masterpiece.

Winchester he attempted to make a stand, but in a battle on May 25 the Confederates had little trouble dislodging the Federals and sending them into headlong retreat. Banks did not stop retreating until he crossed the Potomac the next day, having lost 35 percent of his force.

In Washington, Lincoln and his advisors viewed the situation with alarm, mingled with the shrewd awareness that an opportunity now existed to trap Jackson's entire force. A march of forty miles would place Frémont's 15,000 men at Harrisonburg, eighty miles in Jackson's rear. Lincoln instructed Frémont to make this march. Similarly he ordered McDowell at Fredericksburg to detach 20,000 men and seize Front Royal, a move that would imperil Jackson's line of retreat. The main issue was whether the Union forces could move fast enough to close the trap before Jackson could escape. As Lincoln remarked, it was "a question of legs."

The plan failed. For a variety of reasons, Frémont did not advance into the Valley by the most direct route and instead marched northward for a considerable distance, thereby squandering the best chance to trap Jackson. The Confederate commander managed to elude both Frémont and McDowell. Then he chose a position at Port Republic, a small village where two small streams met to form the south branch of the Shenandoah River.

Spring rains had swollen these streams to the point where they could be crossed only at bridges or rare fords; by controlling the crossings at Port Republic, Jackson could concentrate against either Frémont or McDowell while denying his opponents the opportunity to join forces. Then, in two sharp fights on June 8–9, he bested both rivals. A highly religious man, Jackson exulted to Ewell at the close of the second battle, "General, he who does not see the hand of God in this is blind, sir, blind!"

Whether Ewell viewed it that way is open to question, but military analysts have never had trouble discerning in Jackson's Valley campaign the hand of a master campaign strategist. With an army less than half the size of the forces opposed to him, he had managed to defeat the enemy on five major occasions, hold on to the upper third of the Shenandoah Valley, and above all, force the diversion of thousands of Union troops who might otherwise have joined McClellan's army on the peninsula. His success in the Valley played a crucial role in saving Richmond.

The Failure of Limited War

The modest size of his force notwithstanding, Jackson had already advocated an invasion of the North. He insisted that with 40,000 troops he could do it, and although Lee believed such a venture must await the relief of Richmond, he viewed the idea with interest. Lee reinforced Jackson in hopes that Stonewall might crush the remaining Federals in the Valley. But when no Union forces offered themselves for immediate crushing, Lee changed plans and ordered Jackson to bring most of his troops to Richmond. All possible Confederate forces must be concentrated to defend the capital.

In Lee's mind such a defense could not be passive; a passive defense would allow McClellan the maximum benefit of the powerful artillery in his siege train. Therefore, despite numerical inferiority, the Confederates would have to attack. He knew of Napoleon's successful exploits against larger armies and had witnessed Winfield Scott's triumph over a larger Mexican army. Numbers, in Lee's opinion, were important, but not all-important. Initiative, concentration of force at a decisive point, surprise, and determination counted for at least as much. Good intelligence was also vital. Accordingly, on June 11 he summoned to his headquarters Brigadier General Jeb Stuart, the army's twenty-nine-year-old chief of cavalry. Stuart took 1,200 troopers on a two-day reconnaissance completely around McClellan's army. When he returned he told Lee the Federal right wing was "in the air"—that is, it continued several miles north of the Chickahominy River and then simply ended, anchored to no substantial natural obstacle. Also, McClellan's supplies were still being drawn exclusively from White House Landing on the Pamunkey River. No effort had been made to change the Federal base to a forward point on the James River. Armed with this information, Lee decided to concentrate his army on the exposed Union right flank, break it, then pitch into McClellan's rear and cut his supply line. If successful the Federals would be forced to withdraw the way they had come, back down the peninsula.

The Seven Days

McClellan had five corps east of Richmond—arrayed in a north-south line about five miles east of the city—but only one corps north of the Chickahominy. That force, the V Corps under Brigadier General Fitz John Porter, had the dual mission of screening the Federal base at White House Landing and facilitating a juncture with McDowell's corps should it ever be released by Lincoln from its mission of screening Washington. Lee proposed to use the bulk of his 80,000 available troops to crush Porter and leave only 20,000 to hold the Richmond trenches. It was a daring gamble, but Lee expected McClellan to go on the defensive the moment the Confederate attack opened.

On June 23, 1862, Lee met with his key commanders. Stonewall Jackson was there, having left his troops, then en route to Richmond, and ridden fifty miles to attend the meeting. Lee gave him the vital assignment of turning the right flank of the Union V Corps. Jackson promised to be in position by June 26, and Lee shaped his timetable accordingly. But to everyone's astonishment, Jackson failed to carry out his assignment on time and did not report to headquarters news of his situation or whereabouts. Noon came and went on June 26, and nothing happened. Then at 3 P.M. a division commander, Major General A. P. Hill, decided that the offensive could no longer wait for Jackson. Without asking clearance from Lee, he led his troops straight for the packed cannon of the V Corps. Reluctantly, Lee committed his other divisions to support the charge. Without Jackson to turn the flank, however, his carefully planned offensive degenerated into a brutal frontal assault. Thousands of rebel troops fell to Union rifle and artillery fire

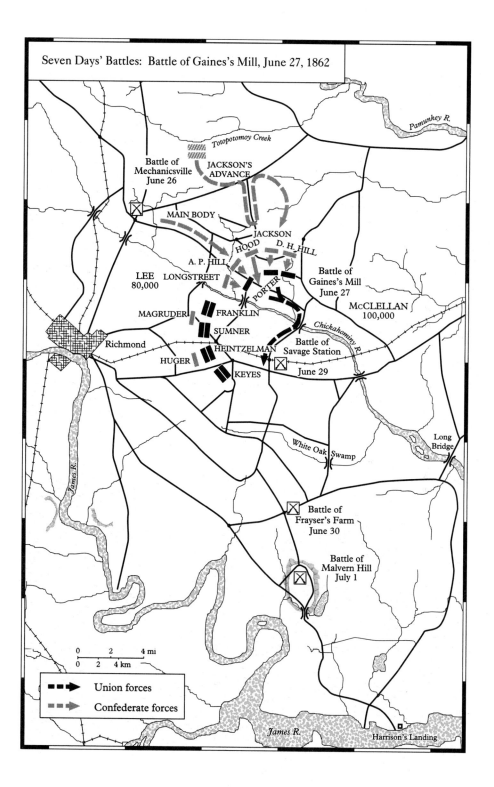

Seven Days' Battles: Battle of Gaines's Mill, June 27, 1862

Pamunkey R.

Totopotomoy Creek

Battle of
Mechanicsville
June 26

JACKSON'S
ADVANCE

MAIN BODY

JACKSON

HOOD   D. H. HILL

A. P. HILL

LEE
80,000

LONGSTREET

PORTER

Battle of
Gaines's Mill
June 27

McCLELLAN
100,000

MAGRUDER   FRANKLIN

Chickahominy R.

SUMNER

Richmond

HUGER   HEINTZELMAN

Battle of
Savage Station
June 29

KEYES

White Oak Swamp

Long
Bridge

James R.

Battle of
Frayser's Farm
June 30

Battle of
Malvern Hill
July 1

0   2   4 mi
0   2   4 km

▪▪▪▶ Union forces

▪▪▪▶ Confederate forces

James R.

Harrison's Landing

without ever piercing the V Corps' formidable positions near Mechanicsville. Worse, the Federals learned of Jackson's belated approach and during the night conducted a skillful withdrawal to even stronger positions at Gaines' Mill, two miles east.

The offensive's second day threatened to be a replay of the first, with much of Lee's force again bludgeoning the Federals in brave but useless charges while Jackson floundered about north of the battlefield. In the afternoon, however, Stonewall finally got his troops into action against the Union right flank, and by dusk the Federals were beaten. Porter successfully withdrew his battered corps south of the Chickahominy. Just as Lee expected, McClellan went over to the defensive. But Lee's own plans never quite worked out. The unfortunate battles at Mechanicsville and Gaines' Mill seemed to set the tone for the entire campaign. Time and again, bad staff work and faulty generalship scuttled spectacular opportunities to maul McClellan's army. Jackson, in strange contrast to his stellar conduct of the Valley campaign, continued to perform poorly—most likely due to the effects of prolonged mental and physical stress.

Still, the victory at Gaines' Mill forced the Federals to abandon their supply base at White House Landing and begin a risky withdrawal south toward a new base along the James River. Lee saw the withdrawal as a chance to demolish McClellan's army completely. But poor intelligence, poor use of artillery, poor tactics and, of course, poor generalship combined to prevent so decisive a result. On June 29 a portion of Lee's army got into a costly but useless fight at Savage Station. The following day saw a botched

The North had good artillery and plenty of it, and when concentrated to deliver massed fire, the results could be devastating. At Malvern Hill on July 1, 1862, Union artillery blasted wave after wave of attacking Confederate infantry. "It was not war," confessed one Southern general, "it was murder."

attempt to envelop the Union army at Frayser's Farm. By July 1, McClellan had nearly made good his withdrawal.

Atop a spacious ridge called Malvern Hill, McClellan deployed much of his field artillery to cover the final stage of his retreat. Swampland on either side of the hill precluded any chance to turn the position, and it appeared much too formidable to be taken by a direct attack. But Lee stubbornly refused to concede McClellan's escape. He ordered a frontal assault. Lines of Confederate soldiers swept forward against the Yankee guns packed along the crest. They were soon shattered as Union artillery tore their ranks to shreds. A Confederate division commander said afterward, "It was not war, it was murder."

But the Seven Days, as the battles between June 26 and July 1 came to be known, resulted in the salvation of Richmond, which was all most Southerners cared about. Lee became a hero. The Army of the Potomac, beaten though not seriously damaged, cowered along the banks of the James at Harrison's Landing. Of the 85,500 Confederates engaged in the battles, 20,141 became casualties, a loss rate of nearly 24 percent. The Federals, by contrast, lost only 15 percent of their own force—15,849 from an army of about 105,000.

A number of historians have since questioned the wisdom of Lee's costly offensive strategy. But the real question is whether he could have saved Richmond in any other way. And the loss of its capital might well have resulted in the Confederacy's political collapse, just as many contemporary observers believed. Even assuming the Confederates were able to relocate their capital and continue the struggle, the loss of Richmond would have opened up the entire eastern Confederacy to further Union attacks. If the South could not successfully defend Virginia, where the gap between sea and mountains was only one hundred miles wide, how could it hope to defend the more open regions farther south?

The End of Conciliation

No sooner did the Army of Northern Virginia dispose of one threat than the Lincoln administration produced another. On June 26, 1862, the Union activated a new "Army of Virginia," composed of three corps under McDowell, Banks, and Frémont, and led by Major General John Pope. Pope came from the war's western theater where he had made a name for himself through the capture of the Mississippi River fortress at Island No. 10. Conceited, pompous, and boastful, he was an easy man to dislike. Soon after assuming command he alienated virtually everyone in his army by issuing a tactless proclamation that seemed a slap in the face to the soldiers who had served in the recent, ill-starred Valley Campaign. The Northern press also derided Pope's broadside.

But Pope soon redeemed himself with a series of draconian orders regarding Virginia civilians. Henceforth, he instructed, the soldiers under his command would live as far as possible off the countryside. They would no longer guard private homes and property. The citizens of occupied territory would be held responsible for guerrilla activity in their midst; the guerrillas themselves would be shot. Persons who refused to take the oath of allegiance would be treated as spies. All in all it seemed clear that Pope intended—as the Northern press put it—to wage war with the kid gloves off.

This sounded a new and increasingly welcome note. Since the beginning of the war most Federal commanders had treated Southern civilians according to the tenets of what was known as the conciliatory policy. This policy assumed that most white Southerners had been hoodwinked into secession by a slaveholding aristocracy, that popular support for the Confederacy was lukewarm at best, and that a program of mild treatment would convince most white Southerners to return to their former allegiance to the United States. As a result, when Union troops first entered Southern territory, they usually promised not to interfere with slavery and to preserve, as far as possible, all constitutional rights. They seldom took food and other supplies from Southern civilians without payment and often furnished guards to protect private homes against intrusion by unruly soldiers.

The Union had no firmer adherent to the conciliatory policy than McClellan. "I am fighting to preserve the Union and uphold its laws," he assured a wealthy Virginia planter, "and for no other purpose." His distaste for the Lincoln administration stemmed, in part, from the conviction that the president was not strong enough to stand up to the pressures for a sterner "war of subjugation" endorsed by the Radical Republicans. When, shortly after the Seven Days' battles, Lincoln came down to Harrison's Landing to visit the Army of the Potomac, McClellan took the occasion to hand the president a letter urging him not to abandon the conciliatory policy. Instead McClellan urged that the government conduct the conflict "upon the highest principles known to Christian Civilization." Private property should be stringently protected and even an "offensive demeanor" by the military toward citizens should receive prompt rebuke. Furthermore, the army should have nothing to do with slavery, "either by supporting or impairing the authority of the master." Lincoln accepted the letter politely. A consummate politician, however, he knew that the time for the limited struggle envisioned by McClellan had run out.

The Drive Toward Emancipation

The war, in any case, had moved beyond conciliation. The major casualty of the shift was slavery. At the war's outset the Lincoln administration had refused to accept any interference with the "peculiar institution," for fear that it would alienate the border states, embitter white Southerners to greater resistance, and alienate many in the North who were willing to support a war for the Union but who rejected fighting to free the slaves. Yet it was clear not only that slavery lay at the root of the struggle but also that the labor of slaves was sustaining the Confederate economy and even being used to construct military fortifications. It was therefore almost impossible for Union troops to battle the Confederacy without disturbing slavery.

Union retreat from Richmond. McClellan's defeat during the Seven Days' battles destroyed the North's hopes for an early victory, scuttled the conciliatory policy, and helped convince Lincoln that the Union could not win the war without attacking slavery.

Indeed, the very presence of Union troops on Southern soil disrupted the stable order on which slavery rested. From the outset, some slaves escaped to Union lines, hoping to gain their freedom. At first—in accordance with orders from Washington—they were returned, but many Northern troops found this policy utterly distasteful. Then, Union Major General Benjamin F. Butler, a former Democratic congressman from Massachusetts, proposed a novel solution to the problem. When a Confederate officer appeared at his headquarters at Fort Monroe, Virginia, demanding the return of several fugitive slaves, Butler rebuffed him. The slaves in question, he said, had been helping to construct Confederate fortifications; as such, he was justified in holding them as "contraband of war." Butler's use of the term was loose, but his argument made excellent practical sense. In early August 1861 the U.S. Congress codified the general principle in its First Confiscation Act, which declared the forfeiture of any slaves used in direct support of the Confederate war effort. The military necessity of such a policy was obvious.

Less obvious was a proclamation issued by Major General John C. Frémont later that month. Then in command of the Department of Missouri and frustrated by the guerrilla warfare in his midst, Frémont decided to free the slaves living in the southern part of the state. Lincoln promptly overruled him. The order was too sweeping, its military purpose unclear. In May 1862, Lincoln overruled Major General David Hunter when Hunter tried the same thing in South Carolina.

Yet by that point Lincoln himself was beginning to move toward a policy of emancipation. In March 1862 he urged Congress to consider a program of compensated emancipation. Six weeks later he signed into law a bill for the compensated emancipation of slaves in the federally regulated District of Columbia. Subsequent legislation ended slavery in the Federal territories—this time without compensation.

Lincoln eagerly waited for the border states to take up his call for compensated emancipation. Their failure to do so profoundly disappointed him. In the meantime, the Peninsula Campaign collapsed and Congress moved toward a harder line, passing a more stringent Second Confiscation Act in July. Lincoln made one final appeal to the congressmen from the border states. When this too failed, Lincoln made his fateful decision to emancipate the slaves by executive order. "We must free the slaves or be ourselves subdued," he told a cabinet member. The slaves were undeniably an element of strength to the Rebels, "and we must decide whether that element should be with us or against us."

On July 22, 1862, Lincoln met with his cabinet and read them a draft of his preliminary Emancipation Proclamation. Most agreed that it was time to issue such a document. The only objection had to do with timing. Secretary of State Seward worried that, given the Union's recent military setbacks, issuing the proclamation immediately would seem like a confession of desperation. Better to wait until a Federal victory. Lincoln saw the logic of this and for the time being put the Emancipation Proclamation aside. In the meantime its existence remained a guarded state secret, while the president waited for a Northern battlefield success.

Confederate Counterstrokes

As it turned out, he had to wait nearly two months. In the meantime McClellan's battered army remained at Harrison's Landing. McClellan asked for 50,000 reinforcements, claiming that with them he could resume

Called "Old Brains," Henry W. Halleck had been a military intellectual in the prewar U.S. Army. As Union general-in-chief from July 1862 to March 1864, he brought greater administrative efficiency to the North's war effort but frustrated Lincoln by his frequent refusal to give field commanders direct orders.

his Richmond offensive. Lincoln considered this pure moonshine. In mid-July he summoned to Washington Major General Henry W. Halleck—his most successful commander to date—and named him general-in-chief. (Since March, when McClellan was relieved of this assignment, the post had been vacant; Lincoln and Stanton had acted, in effect, as the general-in-chief.) Among the first issues Lincoln put to Halleck was what to do with the Army of the Potomac. Although habitually reluctant to make decisions in such matters—he firmly believed that field commanders could best judge their situations—Halleck did little to discourage Lincoln's growing conviction that McClellan's army should be withdrawn. On August 15 the Army of the Potomac began boarding river transports for the return trip. This huge ferrying operation would continue for most of the month.

Meanwhile, in mid-July Pope's new Army of Virginia became active. Pope's mission was threefold: to protect Washington, to ensure Federal control of the Shenandoah Valley, and by operating against the Confederate rail center at Gordonsville, Virginia, to draw Confederate strength from Richmond and thereby divert attention from McClellan. Hindered by the wide dispersion of his forces, his newness to the eastern theater, and his matchless knack for alienating almost everyone, Pope ultimately became the victim of one of Lee's deftest bits of offensive-defensive strategy.

Second Manassas

Lee shaped his planning step by step, constrained by the knowledge that McClellan still lay within striking distance of Richmond. As McClellan's quiescence showed no sign of change, Lee felt assured enough to detach three divisions and send them against Pope's army. These he entrusted to Stonewall Jackson.

On August 9, Jackson fought a preliminary battle against a corps from Pope's army at Cedar Mountain in north-central Virginia. Soon afterward Lee brought most of his army north to join in the struggle against Pope. He knew that McClellan temporarily posed no threat because the Union army had begun its withdrawal from the James River. For nearly two weeks Lee sparred with Pope in the Rappahannock River valley, fruitlessly trying to bring him to bay before McClellan's army reentered the picture.

Lee did not feel strong enough to attack Pope directly, so he elected to maneuver, hoping to cut Pope's communications, threaten Washington, and avoid a general engagement. On August 24 he called Jackson to his headquarters and instructed him to sever the Orange and Alexandria Railroad, Pope's principal line of communications. To accomplish the mission Jackson was given 23,000 troops, leaving Lee with only 32,000 to hold the Rappahannock crossings and fix Pope's attention. Dividing the army violated conventional military wisdom, but Lee saw no alternative. The disparity in numbers between the contending forces rendered the risk unavoidable.

Jackson's execution of the operation gave proof that the military brilliance he displayed in the Shenandoah had not been lost. In a remarkable forced march of fifty-seven miles in two days, Jackson placed his swift

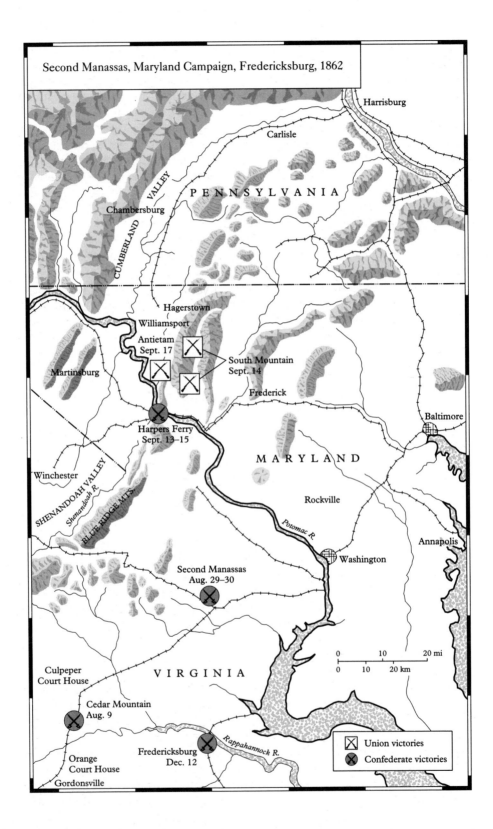

Second Manassas, Maryland Campaign, Fredericksburg, 1862

Harrisburg

Carlisle

P E N N S Y L V A N I A

Chambersburg

CUMBERLAND VALLEY

Hagerstown

Williamsport

Antietam
Sept. 17

South Mountain
Sept. 14

Martinsburg

Frederick

Harpers Ferry
Sept. 13–15

Baltimore

M A R Y L A N D

Winchester

SHENANDOAH VALLEY

Shenandoah R.

BLUE RIDGE MTS.

Rockville

Potomac R.

Annapolis

Washington

Second Manassas
Aug. 29–30

Culpeper
Court House

V I R G I N I A

0   10   20 mi
0   10   20 km

Cedar Mountain
Aug. 9

Orange
Court House

Fredericksburg
Dec. 12

Rappahannock R.

Gordonsville

☒ Union victories
⊗ Confederate victories

infantry—jocularly dubbed his "foot cavalry"—squarely upon Pope's line of communications, cut the Orange and Alexandria Railroad, and demolished a gigantic Union supply depot at Manassas Junction. As a finale, he disappeared into a secluded, defensible position a few miles west of Manassas to await developments.

Aware only that Jackson lurked somewhere in his rear, Pope abandoned his defensive line along the upper Rappahannock River and began beating about the countryside in a disorganized attempt to locate Stonewall's forces. Lee, meanwhile, disengaged from the Rappahannock line as well and began a circuitous march aimed at a juncture with Jackson. Around noon on August 29 the Army of Northern Virginia was reunited as Longstreet's divisions assumed positions just southwest of Jackson's line.

Jackson's troops had been in a fierce battle the day before, and Pope assailed them again early on the 29th. But the Federals were unaware that Longstreet was now in the vicinity. On August 30, still blissfully ignorant of Longstreet's presence, Pope struck Jackson yet again. For a time the rebel situation was critical, but then Longstreet's five divisions broke from their cover and smashed the exposed Union left, sending the Federals in wild retreat until their officers could rally them for a stand on the old Bull Run battlefield. There, repeated Confederate attacks failed to dislodge them. It made no difference. Stung by repeated reverses, Pope elected to withdraw his demoralized forces northeast toward Washington. At a cost of 9,500 men, Lee had inflicted 14,500 casualties upon the Federals and cleared northern Virginia of any major Union army. In twelve weeks of campaigning, Lee had reversed the tide of the war in the east.

Antietam

With Pope beaten and McClellan's army withdrawn behind the Washington fortifications, Lee believed it was time to carry the war from Virginia into enemy country. The Union armies were weakened and demoralized, creating the opportunity to seize the initiative. An advance into Union territory might cause Maryland to secede and perhaps even lead Great Britain and France to grant diplomatic recognition to the Confederacy (although Lee doubted either event would ever occur). Most important, entering enemy territory would permit his army to forage in Maryland and give Virginia the chance to harvest its crops unmolested.

An offensive into Maryland would be difficult for even an army of 200,000, much less Lee's ragged, ill-equipped veterans, now reduced to something less than 50,000. But Lee was developing an almost mystical regard for the prowess of his Confederate soldiers. Time and again he asked them for the impossible, and incredibly, they often gave it to him. He grew convinced that there had never been soldiers like them. He also formed a correspondingly dismal picture of the Union forces and, especially, Union leadership. When a subordinate seemed dubious about his offensive plans, for example, Lee blandly explained that McClellan's caution made them quite practical.

Lee's army crossed the Potomac River on September 4–7. The bands played "Maryland, My Maryland" and the ragged soldiers looked in wonderment at the unspoiled countryside around them. From the outset, however, things went badly. To begin with, Lee expected that his thrust northward into Maryland would force the withdrawal of a 12,000-man Union garrison at Harpers Ferry. The garrison blocked the lower Shenandoah Valley, the avenue by which Lee planned to maintain communications with the South. When the garrison stayed in place, Lee had no choice but to reduce it. After a short stay in Frederick, Maryland, he divided his army into four parts. Three of them, under Jackson's overall command, went after Harpers Ferry. The fourth, consisting of Longstreet's corps and a division under General D. H. Hill, proceeded to the town of Boonsboro to await the operation's completion.

At this point additional problems arose. Unfounded reports of Federal units operating around Chambersburg, Pennsylvania, prompted Lee to divide his army further: D. H. Hill remained at Boonsboro while Longstreet shifted northwest to Hagerstown, Maryland. Jackson's forces took longer than anticipated to get into position. Not until September 13—a full day behind schedule—did they surround Harpers Ferry. Although the town's surrender then became a mere matter of time, it turned out that time was something the Confederates did not have.

Lee had miscalculated McClellan's response to the Maryland invasion. The Virginian had believed it would take three or four weeks for McClellan to reorganize the Union armies defeated at Second Manassas. Instead, McClellan did the job in less than seven days. As Jackson's units sewed up Harpers Ferry, the Army of the Potomac arrived at Frederick, Maryland, just one day's hard march from the scattered Confederate army. The situation would become critical if the Union general realized the exposed state of Lee's army. And that is precisely what occurred.

By incredible coincidence, two Federal soldiers found a copy of Lee's plan for the Harpers Ferry operation in a field outside Frederick. This soon-to-be-famous "Lost Order" quickly went to McClellan, who took one look at it and became understandably ecstatic. "Here," he exulted to one of his generals, "is a paper with which if I cannot whip Bobbie Lee, I will be willing to go home." Unfortunately for the Union cause, McClellan lacked the killer instinct required to capitalize on the situation. Instead of an immediate, rapid advance into the center of Lee's widely divided forces, he sent his columns forward at a leisurely pace. He gave Lee just enough time to retrieve the situation.

Lee heard about McClellan's dangerous advance about midnight on September 13. He issued orders for his troops to occupy the passes of South Mountain, a wooded ridge that formed a barrier between the Union army and his own. The next day three Union corps attacked. Lee's forces managed to fend them off for most of the day, but by evening Lee's hopes for a Northern invasion lay in ruins. From then on he was strictly on the defensive.

Lee probably should have withdrawn across the Potomac River as soon as possible. Initially he planned to do so, but word that Harpers Ferry

Union infantrymen charge through a cornfield at Antietam, September 17, 1862, the bloodiest single day of the war. Though McClellan achieved only a drawn-out battle, Lee was nevertheless forced to abandon his invasion of Maryland. Lincoln issued the Emancipation Proclamation five days later.

was about to surrender emboldened him. He chose instead to withdraw about ten miles west of South Mountain and make a stand at Sharpsburg, Maryland, along the banks of Antietam Creek. The wisdom of this decision is questionable—it meant fighting with a wide river directly in his rear—but Lee's conduct of the battle was magnificent. McClellan advanced slowly, cautiously, giving Lee plenty of time to concentrate most of his army. The Union assault did not come until September 17, and then in a piecemeal fashion that allowed Lee to shift his own outnumbered forces from one threatened point to another. The Army of Northern Virginia held its ground, albeit at tremendous cost: 13,700 casualties out of approximately 40,000 engaged. Union losses totaled 12,350 out of about 87,000 present on the field. This Battle of Antietam had the grim distinction of being the bloodiest single day of the Civil War.

It had another significance as well. Although McClellan missed a spectacular chance to destroy Lee's army, the battle looked enough like a Union victory for Lincoln to follow through on the promise he had made in July. On September 22, 1862, he issued the preliminary Emancipation Proclamation. If the South did not abandon the war by January 1, 1863, he warned, the slaves residing in the rebellious areas would become forever free.

The Emancipation Proclamation irretrievably changed the nature of the war. It outraged Southern opinion, the more so since it conjured fears of the race war white Southerners had always feared. Jefferson Davis considered the proclamation "the most execrable measure recorded in the history

Lincoln's decision to issue the Emancipation Proclamation sparked controversy in the North and outraged the South. In this cartoon penned by a Southern sympathizer living in Baltimore, Lincoln is shown writing the proclamation surrounded by demonic images, his foot planted on the U.S. Constitution.

of guilty man" and for a time considered treating captured Federal officers as inciters of servile insurrection. More than ever, the war had become a struggle to the death.

Bragg's Kentucky Raid

Lee's invasion of Maryland was not the only Confederate offensive during this period. At practically the same time as Lee's Maryland campaign, Confederate forces under Major General Earl Van Dorn tried to recapture the important rail center of Corinth, Mississippi, only to be repulsed on October 4. The Confederate offensive that went farthest and lasted longest, however, was the invasion of Kentucky, masterminded by General Braxton Bragg.

Bragg took over the army (soon to be called the Army of Tennessee) at Tupelo, Mississippi, in mid-June, after Beauregard departed abruptly on sick leave. In many respects Bragg was a most capable officer: energetic, determined, aggressive. He possessed a good strategic mind and sound administrative abilities. It would eventually develop, however, that Bragg possessed equally obvious shortcomings. He had an irascible temperament that alienated many around him, including his chief subordinates. And although decisive, even daring at times, during a crisis he often turned cautious, almost as if he no longer grasped the situation. But until these darker qualities manifested themselves, Bragg looked like a remarkable soldier. Indeed, few campaigns of the Civil War were better conceived and—up to a point—better executed, than Bragg's Kentucky raid.

After his bloodless victory at Corinth and before he became general-in-chief, Halleck dispersed his huge army into two main parts. One part—about 31,000 men under Major General Don Carlos Buell—was ordered east toward Chattanooga, Tennessee, another key railroad town and also the gateway into eastern Tennessee, a bastion of Unionist sentiment. The other, consisting of about 67,000 troops, was scattered about in order to consolidate the Federal grip on western Tennessee. Halleck's questionable disposition drained most of the momentum from his western offensive. When, in mid-July, he went east to become general-in-chief, operational control passed to Buell—now in northern Alabama—and Grant, who commanded the dispersed Union troops in western Tennessee.

Grant needed months to reconcentrate sufficient forces to resume offensive operations. In the meantime Buell, advancing toward Chattanooga, ran into a variety of delays from frequent guerrilla incursions, enemy cavalry raids, and the burden of repairing his lines of supply—the railroads leading east from Corinth and south from Nashville.

Grant's immobility and Buell's glacial movements invited some kind of Confederate riposte. Rejecting the option of an advance toward Grant, Bragg decided to shift his army eastward toward Chattanooga, then join forces with Confederate units in eastern Tennessee and embark on an invasion of Kentucky. In so doing he would turn Buell's flank and force him to retreat—perhaps even to abandon middle Tennessee. The move might also encourage Kentucky to join the Confederacy and fill his army's ranks with thousands of Bluegrass volunteers. Leaving a covering force at Tupelo under Major General Earl Van Dorn, Bragg embarked on this new operation in mid-July.

The shift east required over a month to execute. Bragg sent his infantry to Chattanooga via railroad—a long, circuitous journey that carried them as far south as Mobile, Alabama. Meanwhile his slow-moving artillery and wagon trains traveled by road. As Bragg's army completed its concentration, the Confederates in eastern Tennessee, under Lieutenant General Edmund Kirby Smith, began an advance across the Cumberland Plateau into central Kentucky. By the end of August Kirby Smith had reached Lexington. Bragg then rapidly advanced from Chattanooga and within two weeks stood on Kentucky soil.

This gigantic raid terrified the inhabitants of Illinois, Indiana, and Ohio and briefly installed a pro-Confederate governor at Frankfort, the state capital of Kentucky. It also forced Buell's Union army to abandon northern Alabama, relinquish much of central Tennessee except Nashville, and fall back practically to Louisville, Kentucky, before turning east to deal with Bragg's army. By that time it was early October. Bragg then had about 22,500 veteran troops with him, supported by another 10,000 under Kirby

Battle of Munfordville, Kentucky. While Lee advanced into Maryland, a second Confederate army under Braxton Bragg invaded Kentucky. Bragg hoped thousands of Kentucky men would flock to his forces, but few did. "Their hearts are with us," one Confederate general complained, "but their bluegrass and fat cattle are against us."

Smith. Buell had about 60,000 troops, but his imposing numerical advantage was partially offset by the fact that his army contained many unseasoned troops and its organization was largely improvised.

Neither side fully understood the other's dispositions. The Battle of Perryville that ensued began as a meeting engagement when units from both sides stumbled into one another while searching for fresh water in drought-stricken central Kentucky. The main fight commenced at 2 P.M. on October 8 and continued until well into the night. When it was over, the Federals had lost 845 killed, 2,851 wounded, and 515 captured or missing: a total of 4,211. Confederate casualties numbered 510 killed, 2,635 wounded, and 251 captured or missing—3,396 in all. But although the Rebels inflicted greater losses and held most of the battlefield at day's end, Bragg correctly realized he could not capitalize on the victory. Perryville ended his invasion of Kentucky; he withdrew southward to Murfreesboro, Tennessee.

Autumn Stalemate

In many respects the simultaneous Confederate raids into Maryland and Kentucky in the summer and fall of 1862 represented the military high tide of the Southern cause. Never again would a rebel triumph seem so within reach. By the end of August reports from Great Britain had indicated that the British were starved for cotton, impressed by the Confederacy's resilience, and perhaps on the verge of recognizing the Southern nation. A major Confederate victory at that point might have triggered foreign intervention, just as the American triumph at Saratoga had brought about the French alliance during the War for Independence. The population of the South had felt a rising thrill of expectation; Northerners were correspondingly alarmed and depressed. But the moment ended quickly, and autumn brought only a new round of campaigning.

Fredericksburg

After the Battle of Antietam, McClellan, much to the disgust of the Lincoln administration, tamely kept his army in western Maryland until the end of October 1862. Eventually McClellan crossed the Potomac and headed south toward Warrenton, Virginia, but Lincoln had had enough of his excessive caution and on November 7 relieved him of his command.

McClellan's replacement was Major General Ambrose E. Burnside, an amiable, modest soul who had enjoyed success in amphibious operations against the Carolina coast. When offered command of the Army of the Potomac, he tried to decline the job because he felt unequal to the responsibility. Although events would swiftly and amply prove him correct, at the outset he did rather well.

Within a week of assuming command, Burnside started the Union army on a new "On to Richmond" campaign. This one aimed at sliding past Lee's right flank and crossing the Rappahannock River at Fredericksburg, about fifty miles north of the Confederate capital. Lee had to move rapidly to counter the move; initially he even felt he might have to fall back to a position along the North Anna River, about halfway between Fredericksburg and the capital. Burnside, however, soon lost control of the situation and wound up giving Lee the easiest victory of his career.

Burnside's plans required a prompt crossing of the Rappahannock into Fredericksburg before the Confederates could oppose him in force. Unfortunately for him, the necessary pontoon bridges failed to arrive until well into December, giving Lee ample time to concentrate in and around the town. The Army of Northern Virginia took well-nigh impregnable positions on Marye's Heights just west of the city. Burnside foolishly persisted in his now pointless plan of campaign, and on December 11 two Confederate signal guns announced that the Federals were attempting a crossing.

Lee was unfazed. He wanted the Northerners to attack. With his troops posted on Marye's Heights, defeat was out of the question. The only unknown factor was the ultimate size of the Union casualty list. The entire Army of Northern Virginia had the same absolute certainty regarding the battle's outcome. Longstreet asked one of his artillerists about an idle cannon, only to be told that other Confederate guns already covered the ground so well that its use was academic: "A chicken could not live on that field when we open fire on it."

Lee made no serious attempt to keep the Federals from entering Fredericksburg. On December 13, Burnside made six major assaults against

Marye's Heights. All failed. Massed rebel infantry and artillery scythed them down by the hundreds. The Battle of Fredericksburg ended as it was destined to end—in an inexpensive Confederate victory. The Federals lost over 12,500 men; Confederate losses totaled fewer than 5,500. But the constricted battle area offered Lee no scope for a counterattack. He had to content himself with watching the wounded enemy retire to the river's far bank.

Grant's Overland Campaign Against Vicksburg

Meanwhile in Mississippi, Grant had at last gathered enough of an army to inaugurate a late autumn offensive. His objective was Vicksburg, Mississippi. The city stood on high bluffs at a hairpin turn in the Mississippi River, about three hundred miles downstream from Memphis. After the loss of Columbus, Kentucky, and Island No. 10, Vicksburg became the Confederacy's main fortress on the Mississippi; a second bastion was built at Port Hudson, Louisiana, two hundred miles farther south. Between these two points rebel forces still controlled the river. As long as they did, the Confederacy would remain an unbroken nation stretching from Texas to the Virginia capes; as long as they did, midwestern produce could not be shipped down the Mississippi. Capturing Vicksburg thus became a vital Union goal.

In many respects this task was a general's nightmare. The ideal way to attack Vicksburg would have been to move a large army downriver to within striking distance of the city, supply it by river transports, and then maneuver against the city from the northeast. Geography, however, denied Grant so straightforward a solution. Just north of Vicksburg lay the Yazoo River Delta, a vast stretch of woodlands and swamps. The Delta country sprawled along the eastern bank of the Mississippi for about 140 miles; in places it was forty miles across. No army could hope to operate in such a region. There was really only one point north of Vicksburg from which the city could be attacked, albeit with difficulty, and that was at Chickasaw Bluffs immediately above the town. The Chickasaw Bluffs position, however, combined excellent terrain for the defender with scant maneuvering room for the attacker; this unhappy fact, from the Federal point of view, made it an approach of last resort.

South of Vicksburg the ground was less forbidding than the Delta country but almost as inaccessible. The guns of the fortress made it impossible to transport an army there by river, and if Grant tried to march his troops past the city along the west bank, he would find it impossible to keep the army supplied. An attack directly from the west was out of the question: at Vicksburg the Mississippi was a half-mile wide. That left an attack from the east. But in order to get there, Grant would first have to march his army 250 miles; worse, to supply it he would have to depend exclusively on the Mississippi Central Railroad, a conduit that seemed not only inadequate but mortally vulnerable to interdiction by fast-riding Confederate cavalry.

Still, the overland route seemed the least forbidding prospect and in November Grant set forth with his army, now christened the Army of the Tennessee. Initially everything went smoothly. Lieutenant General John C.

Pemberton, the Confederate commander assigned to defend Vicksburg, fell back before Grant's advance and did not stop until he reached Grenada, Mississippi—about one third of the total distance Grant's men would have to cover. Grant got as far as the town of Oxford, after which the roof caved in. Far back in Tennessee, Confederate cavalry raider Nathan Bedford Forrest led a column of horsemen in a lightning stab that wrecked a good portion of the railroad from which Grant received his supplies. Closer to home, a second raid led by Major General Earl Van Dorn struck Grant's advanced supply base at Holly Springs, Mississippi. Grant had no choice but to withdraw his entire force back to Tennessee.

Even so, the loss of Holly Springs afforded Grant an intriguing lesson. With his military foodstuffs destroyed, Grant instructed his troops to live off the countryside. He hoped they could scrounge enough food to keep body and soul together until they could link up with a regular supply line again. Instead the army not only survived but actually *feasted*. It turned out that this part of the country had a huge food surplus; the men found plenty of hams, corn, poultry, and vegetables. Grant was impressed: in the middle of December, a small corner of the state of Mississippi could feed 40,000 extra mouths. It was something he did not forget.

Simultaneously with Grant's abortive drive down the Mississippi Central Railroad, a second force under Sherman embarked at Memphis and steamed down the Mississippi River to Chickasaw Bluffs, just north of Vicksburg itself. The plan called for Grant's army to distract Pemberton's attention while Sherman made a sudden grab for the city. In the wake of Holly Springs the scheme became a fiasco. Grant's precipitous retreat enabled Pemberton to bring one third of his own men back to Vicksburg. They arrived in plenty of time to bolster the lines at Chickasaw Bluffs, and when Sherman attacked on December 29 he received a crisp rebuff. The year ended with Vicksburg looking tougher to crack than ever.

Stone's River

The same might be said of middle Tennessee. After its withdrawal from Kentucky, Bragg's Army of Tennessee took up position at Murfreesboro, astride the railroad that led from Nashville to Chattanooga. Buell's army came south and occupied Nashville. Meanwhile Lincoln, disenchanted with Buell's lack of aggressiveness, replaced him with a new commander, Major General William S. Rosecrans.

Rosecrans had performed capably in previous operations, possessed good administrative abilities, and enjoyed a strong rapport with his troops, who dubbed him "Old Rosy." But like many Union commanders, he did not like to advance until he felt completely ready, and he spent most of November and December gathering tons of supplies at Nashville. Only on December 26 did he move southeast against Bragg's army at Murfreesboro.

The last dawn of 1862 found Rosecrans's army a few miles west of Murfreesboro with the Confederates drawn up in front of them. Rosecrans planned to attack the rebel right flank; Bragg, however, anticipated him and

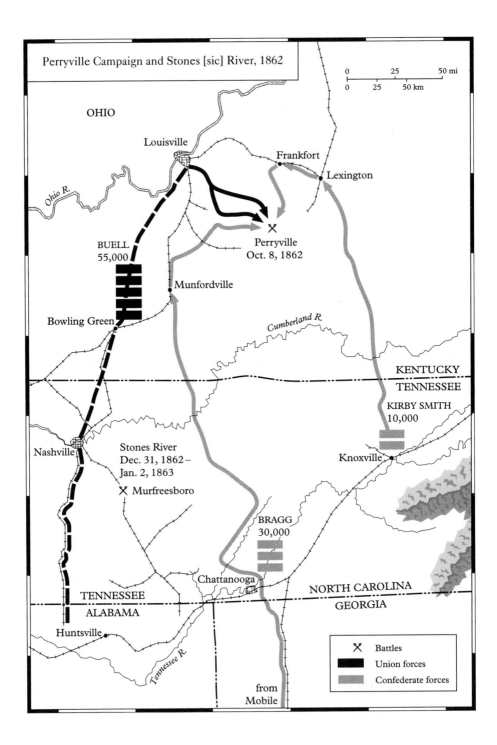

Perryville Campaign and Stones [sic] River, 1862

0   25   50 mi
0   25   50 km

OHIO

Louisville

Frankfort

Lexington

Ohio R.

Perryville
Oct. 8, 1862

BUELL
55,000

Munfordville

Bowling Green

Cumberland R.

KENTUCKY
TENNESSEE

KIRBY SMITH
10,000

Nashville

Stones River
Dec. 31, 1862 –
Jan. 2, 1863

Knoxville

X Murfreesboro

BRAGG
30,000

Chattanooga

NORTH CAROLINA

TENNESSEE
ALABAMA

GEORGIA

Huntsville

Tennessee R.

from
Mobile

X   Battles
    Union forces
    Confederate forces

struck the Union right flank instead. Surprised by the suddenness of the attack and shattered by its weight, the right wing of Rosecrans's army collapsed. By early afternoon the Federal position resembled a jackknife with the blade nearly closed. Only the most desperate fighting saved the Northern army from collapse.

That evening Rosecrans held a council of war and asked his chief subordinates if they thought a retreat in order. His senior corps commander, Major General George H. Thomas, gave the obvious reply: "Hell," he boomed, "this army can't retreat." It was true. The Union situation was so precarious, its sole line of retreat so exposed, that any rearward movement would have quickly dissolved into a rout. Recognizing the logic of this, Rosecrans elected to stand.

New Year's Day of 1863 was quiet as both armies recovered from the previous day's ordeal. Bragg believed he could not press his attack on the Union right flank—his troops in that sector were exhausted and decimated by the vicious fighting there—but neither did he want to give up his hard-won advantage. On January 2, therefore, he ordered his remaining fresh troops to strike the Union left in an attack across Stone's River. This assault, however, delayed until late in the day, was torn apart by Union artillery. With his army now completely worn out, Bragg reluctantly decided to fall back some thirty miles southeast to Tullahoma, Tennessee. The Union army, as shattered by its barren victory as by a major defeat, did not pursue.

☆   ☆   ☆   ☆

Thus the year 1862, which had begun with the belief that a quick and relatively bloodless victory was still possible, ended in military stalemate. From a Union perspective, the military problem of defeating the Confederacy loomed greater than ever. Geography was one factor. In Virginia, the constricted, river-choked arena made it difficult even for large armies to bring their strength effectively to bear. Fredericksburg had shown that. In the west, great distances meant that the Federals had to supply their forces over long, vulnerable lines of supply—a point rammed home by the cavalry raids of Forrest and Van Dorn.

The respective fighting power of the two opponents was a second factor. Although the Federals usually enjoyed a substantial numerical advantage, the rival armies had shown themselves too evenly matched in strength and resilience. Battles like Stone's River suggested that even the most determined, well-executed assaults wrecked the attacker as much as the defender, and although at Stone's River the attackers were Confederates, the onus of offensive warfare still lay chiefly with the North.

A third factor—and from the Federal point of view the most surprising—was the psychological strength of Southern resistance. At the beginning of 1862 most Northerners subscribed to the belief that popular support for the Confederacy was shallow at best. Lincoln doubted whether secessionists formed a majority anywhere except South Carolina and thought that a large, latent Unionist sentiment lay just below the surface, awaiting only a Federal victory to emerge and throw off the Confederate yoke. Thousands of

Northerners shared this conviction, including Ulysses S. Grant. Looking back on this period of the war years later, Grant wrote that until the spring of 1862, he had supposed the Southern people were not in earnest and that one or two decisive Federal successes would make them quit the war. "[Forts] Donelson and Henry," he continued, "were such victories." But when they led only to the furious Confederate counterattack at Shiloh, "then, indeed, I gave up all idea of saving the Union except by complete conquest."

Most Northerners took a bit longer to reach the same conclusion. The turning point, for most of them, was the defeat of McClellan's peninsula campaign. The failure of this campaign turned many Northerners sharply against a limited war directed solely against Confederate armies. Until then, Union policy makers had fought the war somewhat in the manner of the "cabinet wars" of the eighteenth century. Severe clashes could and did occur, but an important goal was to prevent severe disruptions in the fabric of society. Increasingly, however, the American Civil War became a struggle with no holds barred, more so than even the French Revolution and Napoleonic Wars. A Union soldier aptly expressed the new outlook: "I am like the fellow that got his house burned by the guerillas," he wrote. "[H]e was in for emancipation subjugation extermination and hell and damnation. We are in war and anything to beat the south."

The issuance of the Emancipation Proclamation signaled this major change in the conflict. The struggle was no longer one to quell rebellion. It had become what Lincoln initially feared it would become—a "remorseless, revolutionary struggle" to overthrow the institution on which the South's social and economic structure depended. As a result, measures unthinkable in the war's first year—the seizure or destruction of crops and livestock, the demolition of factories, even the burning of towns and villages—now seemed not only permissible but necessary. The stakes of the conflict, already great, increased still further. The Civil War was becoming a total war.

SUGGESTED READINGS

Cozzens, Peter. *No Better Place to Die: The Battle of Stone's River* (Urbana and Chicago: University of Illinois Press, 1990).

Freeman, Douglas S. *Robert E. Lee,* 4 vols. (New York: Charles Scribner's Sons, 1934–1935).

———. *Lee's Lieutenants: A Study in Command,* 3 vols. (New York: Charles Scribner's Sons, 1942–1944).

Hennessy, John J. *Return to Bull Run: The Campaign of Second Manassas* (New York: Simon and Schuster, 1993).

Jones, Archer. *Confederate Strategy from Shiloh to Vicksburg* (Baton Rouge: Louisiana State University Press, 1961).

McDonough, James Lee. *War in Kentucky: From Shiloh to Perryville* (Knoxville: University of Tennessee Press, 1994).

McWhiney, Grady. *Braxton Bragg and Confederate Defeat*, Vol. 1, *Field Command* (New York: Columbia University Press, 1969).

Sears, Stephen W. *George B. McClellan: The Young Napoleon* (New York: Ticknor & Fields, 1988).

———. *To the Gates of Richmond: The Peninsula Campaign* (New York: Ticknor & Fields, 1992).

———. *Landscape Turned Red: The Battle of Antietam* (New York: Ticknor & Fields, 1983).

Tanner, Robert G. *Stonewall in the Valley* (Garden City, N.Y.: Doubleday, 1974).

Vandiver, Frank. *Mighty Stonewall* (New York: McGraw-Hill, 1957).

4

THE CIVIL WAR, 1863:
MOVING DEMOCRACIES
TOWARD TOTAL WAR

The Austerlitz Chimera

Two Societies at War

Vicksburg and Gettysburg

Struggle for the Gateway

The year 1863 saw the conflict's continued evolution into a total war. The North and South had already fielded large armies composed of volunteers, and the South had adopted a conscription law in April 1862. In March 1863 the Union government followed suit with a conscription law of its own. Both sides continued to mobilize their economic resources to support the war and increasingly saw those resources as legitimate military targets. Northern forces in particular began to confiscate or destroy factories, mills, railroads, and agricultural products that might be used to support Southern armies.

The North moved toward such measures in part because breaking the Confederacy's military strength through combat alone had proven impossible. Although slow to recognize it, both sides possessed armies too large and durable to be destroyed in a single great battle—especially when so strongly supported by the full resources of their societies. In this respect the Union and Confederate forces were perhaps even more resilient than their European predecessors. Frederick the Great had tried to apply all the resources of the state to his defense of Prussia, but he had been unwilling to unleash the passions of his people. During the wars of the French Revolution and Napoleon, the French had roused the people, tapped the resources of the entire nation, and raised mass national armies, but they had not gone to the limits of total war. By 1863 both sides in the Civil War were going farther toward total war than Europeans had been willing or able to go. In such a struggle, the larger population and superior economic muscle of the North promised a Union victory—if the political commitment to continue the struggle could be maintained.

It was a big if. When 1863 began, the Confederate leadership still had reason to hope for ultimate victory. The victories at Fredericksburg, Holly Springs, and Chickasaw Bluffs showed the steadiness of Southern valor, while the bloody standoff at Stone's River at least promised continued stalemate. The North, for its part, seemed to be tiring; the autumn elections had resulted in significant gains for the Democrats, many of whom favored a compromise peace. But 1863 proved to be the military turning point of the Civil War; by year's end the tide ran clearly against the South. The Union success occurred in two thunderclaps: first the almost simultaneous triumphs at Gettysburg and Vicksburg in early July, then—after a harrowing ordeal along the Tennessee-Georgia border—a dramatic autumn victory at Chattanooga.

The Austerlitz Chimera

First, however, the Union had to endure a number of humiliations. In January 1863, Burnside tried to redeem himself with a midwinter offensive northwest of Fredericksburg. Torrential rains drowned the operation; soldiers derisively called it Burnside's "Mud March." Then in April a promising cavalry raid in northern Alabama came to grief when pursuing rebel horsemen under Bedford Forrest bagged the entire Union detachment of 2,000 men. The following month the Army of the Potomac—under yet another commander—suffered a major defeat at Chancellorsville, Virginia.

The Quest for Decisive Battle

Perhaps better than any other, the Chancellorsville battle illustrates the mid-nineteenth-century American fixation with the slashing offensive style of Napoleon. Generals commonly issued Napoleonic addresses to their troops and patterned their operations after famous Napoleonic victories. A perennial favorite was the Battle of Austerlitz, fought on December 2, 1805. The reason for the fixation was simple: the name was synonymous with decisive battle. At Austerlitz, Napoleon had routed the Austrian and Russian armies in a single day and secured an armistice from Austria just two days afterward. Austerlitz thus represented the apogee of military art and displayed, as Dennis Hart Mahan, West Point's strategic guru, expressed it, "those grand features of the art [of war], by which an enemy is broken and utterly dispersed by one and the same blow."

To be sure, not every Civil War commander sought an Austerlitz-like victory. On the Union side, Generals Halleck, Buell, McClellan, and Sherman were more concerned with the occupation of strategic places than the destruction of an enemy army in battle. Among Confederates, Joseph E.

Johnston clearly preferred a defensive strategy—his counterstroke at Seven Pines was practically the only major offensive battle of his career. These, however, were exceptional figures. The majority of commanders cherished the vision of a decisive victory over the enemy.

Almost without exception they met disappointment. The possible explanations for this are legion. To begin with, the increased range and firepower of the rifled musket, especially when combined with field entrenchments (which became an increasingly pronounced feature of Civil War battlefields after 1862), gave defenders a greater edge over their attackers. Then too, Civil War armies typically had a fairly low ratio of cavalry to infantry, and without the combination of speed and power embodied in large formations of heavy cavalry it was almost impossible for a victorious army to catch and destroy a retreating opponent. The heavy woodlands and broken terrain characteristic of Civil War battlefields further limited the utility of cavalry in large engagements. Instead both sides used their horsemen primarily for reconnaissance, screening, and raiding. Thus cavalry charges on a Napoleonic scale occurred only rarely. When they did, however—as at Cedar Creek in 1864—they displayed their traditional ability to overtake retreating infantry, shatter a defeated army, and produce a fairly good approximation of Austerlitz.

Another possible explanation focuses on the organizational limitations of Civil War armies, which were, of course, largely officered by citizen-soldiers. One might also suggest that the failure of Civil War generals to achieve a decisive victory reflected, to a considerable degree, their limited military abilities; after all, it took a Napoleon to win the Battle of Austerlitz.

But perhaps the main reason for the dearth of truly decisive Civil War battles was simply that such battles seldom occurred anywhere, at any time. Although greatly sought-after from the time of Gustavus Adolphus onward, a victory "by which an enemy is broken and utterly dispersed by one and the same blow" occurred, at best, on only a half-dozen occasions each century and required an unusual combination of circumstances to produce. Moreover, even a "decisive" battle was seldom decisive in any ultimate sense. Despite their calamitous defeat at Blenheim, for example, the French fought the War of the Spanish Succession for more than a decade; eventually, indeed, they obtained rather favorable terms for peace. And Austerlitz, of course, was followed ultimately by Leipzig and Waterloo.

Thus to the extent that Civil War commanders quested after decisive battle, they largely pursued a mirage. The Chancellorsville campaign prominently displayed both the seriousness of this quest and its attendant pitfalls and frustrations.

Chancellorsville: Act One

In late January 1863, after his abortive "Mud March," Burnside was replaced as commander of the Army of the Potomac by Major General Joseph Hooker. Although considered an ambitious opportunist, Hooker was also a combative, competent soldier. With astonishing speed and deftness he restored the flagging morale of the Army of the Potomac, largely by improving rations and camp sanitation and by introducing the corps badges that were the prototypes for modern unit patches. Then he prepared for another offensive.

The Army of the Potomac wintered at Falmouth, Virginia, just across the Rappahannock River from Lee's army at Fredericksburg. As the spring of 1863 approached, Hooker formulated an operations plan based largely on the ideas of Montgomery C. Meigs, the Union army's quartermaster general. Meigs had earlier written that "what is needed is a great and overwhelming defeat and destruction of [Lee's] army." His solution was a bold, rapid turning movement around the Confederate left flank—"such a march as Napoleon made at Jena, as Lee made in his campaign against Pope"—with the objective of gaining the Confederate rear. If, Meigs counseled, "you throw your whole army upon his communications, interpose between him and Richmond . . . and he fights, if you are successful, he has no retreat." This was nothing if not the dream of a decisive Napoleonic victory.

Hooker embraced Meigs's plan and also adopted Meigs's additional suggestion to supplement the turning movement by unleashing cavalry against Lee's lines of communication. But he decided to use only a bit more than half his army for the turning movement. The remainder would confront and fix Lee at Fredericksburg. With any luck this second force would distract the Confederates while Hooker made his march. Later, with Union forces established firmly on Lee's flank, Hooker could launch an offensive, and Lee's army could be crushed between the two halves.

Hooker had more than enough troops to do the job: about 110,000 in all. In mid-April a large cavalry force set forth on a major raid against the railroads that linked Lee's army with Richmond. Then on April 28, Hooker placed his great enveloping column in motion. Early next morning Union Major General John Sedgwick, entrusted with the task of fixing Lee, began crossing the Rappahannock River below Fredericksburg under cover of a heavy fog.

Lee's scouts soon brought him word of this latter movement. Word also came from Jeb Stuart of another crossing at Kelly's Ford, some twenty-five miles to the northwest. By evening Lee knew Hooker's main body had forded the Rapidan River and that two large Federal forces threatened him front and rear. Lee had just 59,500 troops with which to oppose an enemy almost twice that size. In effect, Hooker had prepared a gigantic trap for Lee, and conventional wisdom dictated a quick withdrawal before its jaws could spring shut. Lee, however, seldom thought conventionally. He correctly perceived that Sedgwick's thrust was largely a diversion; the situation as a whole was simply his big chance to hit Hooker's army while it was divided.

For the next two days Lee weighed alternatives, finally deciding to concentrate against Hooker's main body. Leaving 10,000 Confederate troops under command of Major General Jubal Early to watch Sedgwick, Lee moved west into the thickets around Chancellorsville, a crossroads eleven miles west of Fredericksburg surrounded by a dense second-growth forest known locally as the Wilderness. Jeb Stuart's cavalry, meanwhile, performed valuable scouting functions and prevented Hooker from finding out much about Lee's forces. By the evening of May 1, Lee knew two important things about the Union army. First, Hooker had stopped advancing. His men were felling trees to reinforce defensive fieldworks, which implied a temporary halt in the Federal offensive. Second, the extreme right of Hooker's army lay "in the air," anchored to no natural obstacle and so inviting attack.

Chancellorsville: Act Two

As a pallid moon rose over the gloomy Wilderness thickets, Lee and Jackson settled down to plot their next move. They conferred for several hours, finally deciding that Jackson would march 28,000 men across Hooker's front and strike that exposed right flank. Lee, meanwhile, would use his 14,000 remaining troops to dupe Hooker into thinking he intended a frontal assault.

As in the Seven Days, if the Union commander realized the true state of affairs, he could turn Lee's gamble into a catastrophe. But in Lee's reckoning Hooker's construction of fieldworks indicated an abdication of the initiative. And whereas Lee had retained his own cavalry to serve as the eyes of the army, Hooker had detached his own to operate against the Confederate supply lines. The Union commander therefore lacked the intelligence-gathering force necessary to grasp sudden changes in the operational picture.

Jackson's flank march did not go off without a hitch. It began three hours late and was not carried off in complete secrecy. Union pickets spotted Jackson's column as early as 9 A.M. By early afternoon scattered musketry betrayed skirmishing between Federals and Confederates along the line of march. Hooker, however, reacted cautiously and Jackson refused to panic. Despite a foray made by a venturesome Union corps against his artillery trains, Jackson continued his advance and by 5:15 P.M. had drawn up his forces astride the Orange Turnpike, west of Chancellorsville, and faced them almost due east. Ahead lay the exposed flank of the Union XI Corps, partially alerted but still largely unprepared.

Jackson gave the order. Suddenly the gnarled thickets filled with the rebel yell and the Confederates went crashing forward in the diminishing light. The XI Corps attempted to make a stand, with units here and there rallying in an attempt to stem the rebel tide, but their tactical situation was hopeless. Jackson pumped additional divisions into the fight as soon as they arrived. Within three hours, the Confederates had driven forward two miles, folding Hooker's lines into a "U" centered upon the large, isolated house called "Chancellorsville," which gave the clearing and battlefield its name. There resistance stiffened, and the Confederate attack lost momentum in the gathering darkness.

Jackson, accompanied by a cavalcade of staff officers, rode forward to reconnoiter. A band of North Carolina troops mistook his party for Union cavalry and opened fire, wounding him dangerously in the left arm. Compounding the mishap, Jackson's senior division commander fell to enemy fire at almost the same moment. Not until midnight did a

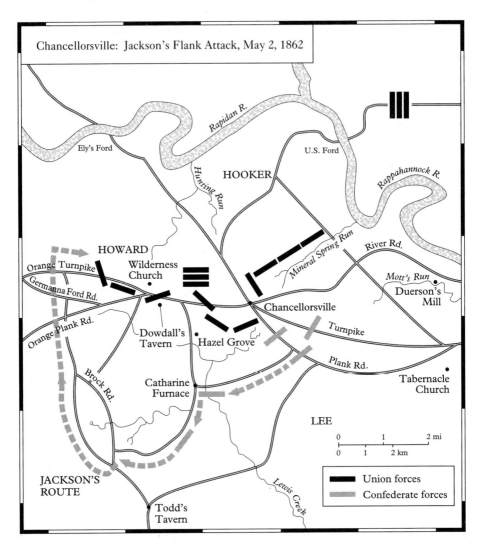

Chancellorsville: Jackson's Flank Attack, May 2, 1862

Rapidan R.

Ely's Ford

U.S. Ford

Rappahannock R.

HOOKER

Hunting Run

HOWARD

Mineral Spring Run

River Rd.

Orange Turnpike

Wilderness Church

Mott's Run

Duerson's Mill

Germanna Ford Rd.

Chancellorsville

Orange Plank Rd.

Turnpike

Dowdall's Tavern

Hazel Grove

Plank Rd.

Brock Rd.

Catharine Furnace

Tabernacle Church

LEE

0   1   2 mi

0   1   2 km

JACKSON'S ROUTE

Lewis Creek

Union forces

Confederate forces

Todd's Tavern

replacement, Jeb Stuart, assume command of Jackson's corps, and Stuart had almost no idea of Jackson's plans to continue the attack.

Attacks against Hooker's main body continued throughout May 3 without great success. The psychological blow had already been dealt, however. By noon Hooker withdrew his force into an enclave north of Chancellorsville. Meanwhile, Sedgwick's wing at Fredericksburg had shoved aside Early's 10,000 and was moving west at last. But an afternoon counterattack at Salem's Church, about three miles west of Fredericksburg, blunted his advance.

Lee realized he had to turn his full attention to this other threat. Leaving 25,000 troops under Stuart to contain Hooker, the general threw the rest of his army against Sedgwick's two corps. The Confederates, however, could not get into attacking positions until the afternoon of May 4. Sedgwick used the delay to withdraw to safety beyond the Rappahannock.

The Civil War's most famous military partnership was that between Robert E. Lee and Stonewall Jackson. Shown here in a romanticized postwar print, they plan the smashing flank attack that defeated the Union army at Chancellorsville—and cost Jackson his life.

Subsequently, on May 5 Lee again concentrated against Hooker and planned an assault for the following day.

This last decision reflected a tremendous stubborn streak in Lee, for Hooker had plenty of time to prepare his lines against precisely the frontal assault Lee was so determined to make. The implications were stunning: Lee seriously planned to attack an entrenched army numerically superior to his own. He seemed utterly resolved to wreck Hooker's force and blind to the fact that it simply could not be done. Fortunately for the Army of Northern Virginia, the Federals withdrew during the evening. Daybreak found them safely across the Rappahannock. Lee, enraged, vented his wrath against the general who brought the unwelcome news. "Why, General Pender," he said, "That is what you young men always do. You allow those people to get away. I tell you what to do, but you don't do it. Go after them," he added furiously, "and damage them all you can!"

Hooker, however, had long since moved out of reach. It remained only to tally the losses: 13,000 Confederate casualties this time against a total of 17,000 Federals. The Army of Northern Virginia had won again, but had absorbed 20 percent casualties in the process—losses the South could ill-afford. Nor could it replace one loss in particular. On May 10, Stonewall Jackson died of complications following the removal of his wounded arm. For the rest of the war, Lee had to do without the one subordinate who could make his audacious strategies take fire.

At Chancellorsville both commanders had tried—unsuccessfully—to achieve a Napoleonic decisive victory. In the case of Hooker this could be explained simply by a singular failure of nerve. "I just lost confidence in Joe Hooker," the Union general later admitted. The reasons for Lee's failure were obviously more complex. Some historians have maintained that, except for Jackson's tragic wounding, the Confederate counteroffensive would have cut Hooker off from the Rapidan crossings and destroyed that half of the Union army. Such an outcome seems unlikely; it is certainly unprovable. More impressive is the fact that the Federals were able to restore their front fairly rapidly, despite one of the best-executed flank attacks of the war. Rifled muskets and concentrated artillery helped; so did field fortifications. Then too, there was the usual dearth of heavy cavalry: Stuart had plenty of horsemen available for scouting purposes, but nowhere near enough to launch a major attack. The countryside was far too wooded and broken for a mounted charge to succeed anyway. Finally, the Confederate attackers typically suffered heavy casualties and lost cohesion, so that it was difficult to maintain the momentum of attack. In short, despite Hooker's ineptness and Lee's tactical virtuosity, the Confederates failed to achieve anything like an Austerlitz. The Chancellorsville campaign ended with the strategic situation in Virginia virtually unchanged, except that thousands of homes, North and South, had been plunged into mourning.

Two Societies at War

More often than the wars of the French Revolution and Napoleon, the Civil War is called the first total war. In common with the wars from 1792 to 1815, the Civil War encompassed the complete, or near-complete, mobilization of the belligerents' population and resources to fight an enemy. But it went further and also involved the complete, or near-complete, application of violence against that enemy—violence exerted not only against his military force but also against the civilian society that sustained it. Though one could quibble endlessly about whether the North and South mobilized completely, a large percentage of the population and the economy on both sides was bound up in the war effort. And by mid-1863, Federal armies began large-scale operations aimed at the destruction of Southern war resources and, at least to some degree, the demoralization of Southern civilians.

For both sides the problem of mobilization was similar. Each government had to find ways to generate sufficient military manpower, to clothe, equip, and transport its armed forces, and—somehow—to find a way to pay for it all. The magnitude of these tasks was completely unprecedented in American history, but both governments approached them in generally similar ways and, in both cases, with fairly good success.

The Move to Conscription

At first, both the Union and the Confederacy relied upon volunteers to man their armies. This was the traditional American method and politically the only thinkable one in societies that venerated individual liberty and unobtrusive government. Eventually, however, both sides encountered difficulties in securing enough manpower. The South was the first to feel the pinch. By early 1862 volunteering in the Confederacy had fallen off dramatically, while at the same time a string of Federal successes threatened the new nation with early defeat. Spurred by a sense of impending doom, on April 16, 1862, the Confederate Congress passed the first general conscription act in American history (local conscription had been used during the Colonial Wars and the American Revolution). The act made every able-bodied white male between the ages of 18 and 35 liable for military service.

This bill, however, contemplated a very different sort of conscription from the system employed by the French in 1793. Whereas in Europe

A Northern recruiting office. Like the Confederacy, the Union government secured most of its military manpower through volunteers. But by early 1863 voluntary enlistments had dropped off and many Northern communities offered cash rewards, called "bounties," if men agreed to enlist.

governments used conscription to raise new troops, the Confederate Congress invoked it principally as an incentive for veteran troops to reenlist. Since many of them had signed up for only twelve months, their enlistments were expiring and they might return to civilian life. The Confederate conscription act provided that if the men stayed in the army they could remain in their current units, but if they left they could be drafted and assigned to a new, unfamiliar unit.

As the war continued, however, the Confederate government refined the conscription act so that it became a way to raise new troops as well as encourage veteran soldiers to remain in the ranks. And in February 1864 the Confederate Congress passed a new, more stringent conscription act that declared all white males between 17 and 50 subject to the draft.

The Union government also moved toward conscription, albeit more slowly. In July 1862 the U.S. Congress took the first step when it passed a new Militia Act, authorizing the president to set quotas of troops to be raised by each state and giving him power to enforce the quota through conscription if a given state failed to cough up enough volunteers. But not until March 1863 did the Federal government pass a true draft act, making all able-bodied males between 20 and 45 liable for military service.

In both the North and South, conscription was wildly unpopular, partly because it represented an unprecedented extension of government power into the lives of individuals, but also because of the inequitable way in which it was administered. For example, initially the Confederate Congress permitted a conscript to hire someone to serve in his place. The practice was abolished when the price of a substitute soared beyond $5,000; in the meantime, however, hiring substitutes convinced many ordinary Southerners that the Confederacy's struggle was "a rich man's war and a poor man's fight." Even more upsetting was the so-called "Twenty Negro Law" that exempted one white man for every twenty slaves. This meant that the sons of wealthy plantation owners could be exempted, and even if few men actually took advantage of the law, it contributed to the sense of conscription's unfairness. In the North, the conscription act also permitted the hiring of substitutes; moreover, any man who paid a $300 commutation fee could receive exemption from any given draft call. Ironically the commutation fee, designed to keep the cost of hiring a substitute from soaring out of reach, was intended to help the average man. Instead it only fueled a sense that the draft law was rigged in favor of the wealthy.

In the North, well-to-do communities also frequently raised bounty funds to encourage volunteering, so that their own citizens could elude the draft. Under this system, a man willing to enlist received a cash payment totaling hundreds of dollars. As the war went on and volunteers became harder to find, such bounties increased prodigiously. They soon generated a phenomenon called "bounty-jumping," whereby men went from place to place, enlisted, took their bounties, and then absconded at the first opportunity. One bounty jumper claimed to have done this thirty-two times.

The indirect way in which Civil War conscription operated makes it difficult to assess its effectiveness. It almost certainly encouraged enlistments and, particularly in the South, kept veteran soldiers in the ranks; one

Men of the 107th U.S. Colored Troops. Lincoln's emancipation policy paved the way for the North to begin active recruiting of African-American soldiers.

estimate credits the system with augmenting Union troop levels by 750,000. But the number of men actually drafted was surprisingly small. In the North, barely 46,000 conscripts actually served in the armies. Another 116,000 men hired substitutes, while 87,000 others paid the $300 commutation fee. Between conscripts and substitutes, the Union draft furnished only 6 percent of the North's military manpower. The Confederacy did little better. The available evidence, while incomplete, suggests that roughly 82,000 Southerners entered the army through conscription—about 11 percent of total enlistments.

The political costs of conscription, however, were dramatic. Many Southerners eluded the draft and fought off the enrollment agents who came to conscript them. In some states, especially Georgia and North Carolina, governors who opposed the draft used loopholes in the conscription acts to exempt as many of their citizens as possible. In the North, a number of provost officers lost their lives while attempting to enforce the draft. The worst violence occurred in New York City in July 1863 when angry mobs attacked draft offices, roughed up well-dressed passersby ("There goes a $300 man"), and slaughtered dozens of free blacks, whom they blamed for the war and hence for conscription. All in all, at least 105 people died in the New York City Draft Riot, making it the worst such incident in American history.

Fifty years later, when the United States resorted to the draft in order to fight World War I, officials studied the weaknesses of Union conscription. The result was a much more effective and politically palatable system, since they were able to avoid many pitfalls. In sum, although conscription as practiced in the Civil War filled some of the urgent need on both sides for military manpower, it proved to be an almost textbook case in how not to do it.

The War Economies

Both sides did better at managing their economies, although here again the distended nature of mid-nineteenth-century American society limited what they could accomplish. The Confederate government never achieved a realistic fiscal policy. It passed only a very inadequate income tax, amounting to just one-half of one percent. Instead the Southern leadership financed the war largely through borrowing and by printing fiat money, expedients that eventually spawned a whopping 9,000 percent inflation rate. In April 1863 it also initiated a wildly unpopular "tax-in-kind," by which Confederate agents could seize 10 percent of the goods produced by a given farm or business concern.

Of the two adversaries, the Union tended to perform best, partly because it had a greater population and resource base, and partly because its financial management was much superior to that of the Confederacy. The Lincoln administration's fiscal system was created and managed by Secretary of the Treasury Salmon P. Chase. While it too relied primarily on bonds and paper money, it levied a more extensive income tax, and inflation remained under control in the North. Where the Confederacy generated a mere 5 percent of its revenue through direct taxation, the Federal government managed 21 percent. The South underwrote only about 40 percent of its war expenses through bonds, against 67 percent for the North.

The Lincoln administration managed its war economy principally through alliances with the business community. Cooperation, not coercion, was the preferred mode of operation, and usually it worked very well. For example, although Lincoln quickly secured the legal authority to seize railroads and run them directly in support of the war effort, in practice he relied on Northern railroad men voluntarily to "do the right thing." Only on rare occasions did the Federal government assume overt control of the railroads. Similarly, the Union government constructed no munitions or equipage factories of its own, but rather relied upon a wide array of civilian contractors. And it depended on financiers to make its war-bond program a success.

Ironically, given its commitment to limited government, the Confederate government pursued a much more direct, centralized management of the economy. President Jefferson Davis persuaded Congress to assume control of the telegraph network, to construct new railroads for military purposes, and even to assume direct control of the railroads from private hands. He also urged Congress to encourage and engage in the mining and manufacture of certain essential materials. Congress eventually passed a law that offered inducements to potential manufacturers of such strategically important goods as saltpetre, coal, iron, and firearms. The government set up its own salt works in Louisiana, and the Ordnance Department established a large weapons-building empire. By the end of the war, in fact, the Confederate South had become—in theory at least—one of the most relentlessly centralized nations on earth. World War I would force some European nations to do the same. But the Union example of an alliance between business and government would prove an equally viable—and more effective—means to the same end.

Wartime Resentments

Modern wars often begin with a wave of patriotic outpouring that temporarily drowns dissent. Sooner or later, however, the dissent resurfaces, and a wartime government must master it or perish. For the Union and Confederacy, dissent began early and grew steadily worse as the war progressed. Both governments proved up to the challenge. The Lincoln administration suspended the writ of habeas corpus where necessary, held, at one time or another, an estimated 13,000 political prisoners, and occasionally suspended publication of hostile newspapers. The Confederate government also suspended the writ of habeas corpus and waged an unremitting campaign of repression against the Unionist sympathizers in its midst, most notably in east Tennessee. The imperatives of total war thus impinged not only on the battlefield and the economy, but also on personal liberties.

In the North, the main opposition came from a faction known as the Peace Democrats—derisively nicknamed "Copperheads" by their opponents. They believed that the Federal government could never achieve reunion through force; they also argued that the horrors of civil war, coupled with the constitutional abuses of the Lincoln administration, were far worse than permitting the South to go its own way. A second group of Democrats, called "Legitimists," supported the war but balked at the Lincoln administration's handling of it, particularly its decision to make emancipation a war aim. Then too, the lower parts of Illinois, Indiana, Ohio, and Maryland contained many persons of Southern ancestry, some of whom were Confederate sympathizers.

The South had troubles of its own. To begin with, a substantial number of Southerners bitterly despised the Confederate government. The fact that 100,000 white Southerners actually fought for the Union underscores this point. The South also contained a large, restive slave population which might at any moment rise up and attack its masters. Oddly enough, a good many planters also disliked the Confederate experiment, for the war effort required too many sacrifices from them: impressment of livestock, the conscription of slave labor, the confiscation of cotton, and so on.

Finally, the unexpectedly massive degree to which the Confederate government eventually intervened in the economy alienated many

Southerners. By 1864, three years of war had precipitated what one historian has termed a "revolt of the common people." Ordinary Southerners resented the loss of labor manpower, particularly among nonslaveholders, who had no one to work the land once their able-bodied young men went off to fight. They were also antagonized by the frequent impressments and requisitions of crops, forage, and horseflesh. Class resentment also surfaced. Wealthy families did not suffer privation to the same degree as the poor. The paying of substitutes to avoid conscription was not abolished until 1864.

Thus both the Union and the Confederacy contained large cores of dissent, each with the potential to undermine the war effort. In the North, political success by the Peace Democrats could, at best, impede the vigorous prosecution of the war and, at worst, force a compromise peace. In the South, the "revolt of the common people" threatened to create a condition in which disobedience to the Confederate government could become not only respectable but rampant. If that occurred, a hostile population might encourage deserters, shield them from Confederate authorities, and block efforts to secure the supplies needed to feed and sustain Southern armies. The solution, in each case, was military success. Continued stalemate, especially if punctuated by Confederate victories, benefited the South and kept its dissenters in check. The Lincoln administration, for its part, required tangible evidence of military progress; otherwise the pressures for a compromise peace might prove overwhelming. The harnessing of popular sentiment to the state, made possible by the democratic revolutions, thus proved a two-edged sword for policy makers. It enabled them to tap manpower and economic resources in unprecedented ways. But it also forced them to accommodate popular passions. Thus like many other leaders in the age of mass politics, Lincoln and Davis found themselves riding a tiger.

A Destructive War

As each society mobilized ever more thoroughly to carry on the war, it began to seem necessary to strike not only the enemy's armies but also his economic base. Railroads, factories, mills, and cotton gins, as well as crops and livestock, increasingly became the targets of military operations. To some extent both sides embarked on a program of economic destruction, but of the two the North had both the greater need and the greater opportunity to attack the enemy's war resources.

Some Northerners had urged such attacks from the very outset of the war, but the logic of the conciliatory policy had argued persuasively against a campaign of unbridled destruction. The issuance of the Emancipation Proclamation, however, had signaled the demise of conciliation, and by early 1863 Union policy makers increasingly realized that more destructive measures were necessary. As Halleck explained to Grant in March 1863, "The character of the war has now very much changed within the last year.

There is now no possible hope of reconciliation with the rebels. . . . We must conquer the rebels or be conquered by them." Spurred by this grim logic, some Northern commanders began to claim the full extent of the destruction permissible within the existing rules of war. They were driven to this extreme not only by the changed political equation but even more importantly by their need to supply themselves and, by extension, to deny supplies to the enemy.

Attacks on the South's economic base initially arose from the practice of widespread foraging. Such foraging occurred first in the western theater, where Union armies often found themselves operating in areas where suitable rail and water communications were unavailable. When that occurred, normal supply lines proved inadequate, and Union armies had to augment their official rations with crops and livestock taken directly from local farmers. This foraging soon made them very aware that Confederate forces also drew supplies from the countryside, and western armies began a policy of destroying unneeded crops in order to prevent the Confederates from using them.

For a considerable period large-scale foraging and supply-denial policies remained mainly confined to the western theater. Union armies in the east, it turned out, were far slower to adopt similar policies. This was probably because they were much less successful than their western counterparts at capturing Southern territory. Thus their supply lines simply never lengthened. Since eastern armies seldom experienced serious logistical problems, they underestimated the impact supply denial might have on the enemy. It seldom occurred to them to destroy those supplies at their source, despite the fact that the Southern forces in the east drew considerable food and forage from local districts. Western armies, by contrast, had far greater sensitivity to logistical matters.

Extensive foraging, Union commanders recognized, inevitably meant hardship for civilians. Commanders attempted to minimize such hardship by forbidding abuses and by issuing instructions that Southern families should be left enough supplies for their own use. Even so, civilians suffered a great deal. Partly in an attempt to justify the hardship thus inflicted, Union commanders began to see it as a form of punishment. Eventually they deliberately sharpened the effects of foraging in order to produce political effects: for example, by stripping crops as much as possible from the farms of known secessionist sympathizers.

The next logical step in supply denial was to destroy the mills that processed agricultural products and the railroads that transported them, as well as factories that manufactured militarily useful goods. Destruction of this sort had occurred on a modest scale even during the early months of the war. Nevertheless the year 1863 marked a significant watershed, for it was during that year that one can see the emergence of large-scale destruction carried out, in fairly routine fashion, by large bodies of troops. By mid-1863, then, both sides were trying to mobilize fully to prosecute the war, and the North, at least, had embarked on a program of economic warfare. The Civil War had truly become a total war.

Vicksburg and Gettysburg

In April 1863 a mob of housewives, furious that they could not find enough to feed their families, rioted in the streets of Richmond. The incident underscored a serious disturbance in Confederate morale, born of privation and endless casualty lists, that would only grow worse without some decisive victory to offset it. The win at Chancellorsville a few weeks later was encouraging but incomplete. The Federal Army of the Potomac had retired intact to lick its wounds; it would surely resume the offensive within a few months. Out west the situation had grown disquieting: Grant's army had come down the Mississippi River, cast about for a viable means to attack the fortress city of Vicksburg, and discovered one late in April.

Vicksburg

After the failure of his overland campaign in the fall of 1862, Grant had brought most of his army to Milliken's Bend, a bleak piece of bottomland a few miles north of Vicksburg. Although Grant was now much closer geographically to the Confederate fortress, the biggest operational problem remained unsolved: how to get into a position from which the bastion could be attacked successfully. From January through April he tried a number of alternatives. First his engineers attempted to connect a series of creeks, old river channels, and bayous into a waterway that would enable Union vessels to get around Vicksburg to the south, after which Grant would march his army down and have those vessels ferry him across the river to the dry ground on the eastern shore. This scheme became known as the Lake Providence Route, after its central feature, but after weeks of backbreaking labor the project was abandoned. Next, hundreds of troops and escaped slaves attempted to dig a canal across the neck of the great river bend directly opposite Vicksburg in hopes of changing the course of the Mississippi so that its main channel would bypass the city. This project sparked the imagination of many people—Lincoln expressed particular fascination with the idea—but it failed as well. A third attempt—similar in concept to the Lake Providence Route—called for creating a waterway through the Yazoo Delta country via Steele's Bayou. It produced the spectacle of Union gunboats steaming through a narrow channel in what amounted to a huge flooded forest, but constant harassment by Confederate snipers eventually forced its abandonment. A fourth effort aimed at creating a waterway running down from the Yazoo Pass at the northern end of the Delta. This too failed when the Confederates erected a fort to block it.

Four attempts, four failures—yet Grant was not discouraged. Later he would claim that he never expected these efforts to yield results and agreed to them largely in order to occupy his men and create the illusion of action—an illusion necessary to allay his critics in the North while he

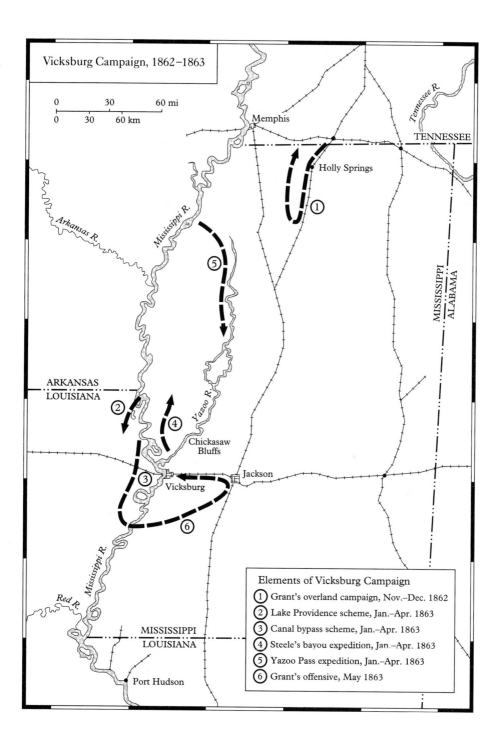

Vicksburg Campaign, 1862–1863

0   30   60 mi
0   30   60 km

Tennessee R.

Memphis

TENNESSEE

Holly Springs

①

Arkansas R.

Mississippi R.

⑤

MISSISSIPPI
ALABAMA

ARKANSAS
LOUISIANA

②

④

Yazoo R.

Chickasaw
Bluffs

③

Jackson

Vicksburg

⑥

Mississippi R.

Red R.

MISSISSIPPI
LOUISIANA

Port Hudson

Elements of Vicksburg Campaign
① Grant's overland campaign, Nov.–Dec. 1862
② Lake Providence scheme, Jan.–Apr. 1863
③ Canal bypass scheme, Jan.–Apr. 1863
④ Steele's bayou expedition, Jan.–Apr. 1863
⑤ Yazoo Pass expedition, Jan.–Apr. 1863
⑥ Grant's offensive, May 1863

Grant confers with Admiral David D. Porter during the campaign against Vicksburg, the Confederacy's bastion on the Mississippi River. Close army-navy cooperation was indispensable to the Union victory there in July 1863.

concocted a plan that would work. By early April he had done it. The ensuing campaign sealed his reputation as a great commander.

On the night of April 16, Admiral David Dixon Porter, the naval officer in charge of the riverine flotilla cooperating with Grant's army, led some of his vessels on a midnight run directly past the guns along the Vicksburg bluffs. Darkness shielded Porter's vessels part of the way; even after the Confederates spotted them and opened fire, the Union boats escaped with the loss of only one transport. More steamers made the dash five nights later. Once below the Vicksburg batteries, Porter's fleet awaited the arrival of Grant's army, which took barges and shallow-draft steamers through a series of bayous that wound past Vicksburg on the Louisiana side of the river. That done, Grant's troops began crossing the Mississippi at Bruinsburg, fifty miles south of Vicksburg, on April 30.

The landing at Bruinsburg placed Grant's army squarely between Vicksburg and the secondary river fortress of Port Hudson, Louisiana. Forty miles eastward lay Jackson, the state capital, and a point at which four railroads converged. One of these led to Vicksburg and formed the bastion's main line of supply. If Grant meant to seize Vicksburg, he would first need to choke off those supplies; for that reason Jackson became his first important objective. Yet to march upon Jackson necessarily meant exposing his own line of supply to ruinous interdiction from Pemberton's army at Vicksburg. Consequently, Grant decided to maintain no supply line at all. Just as his troops had done after the disastrous raid upon Holly Springs in December 1862, they would live off the country, except that this time the choice was deliberate.

At the beginning of May his three army corps headed east, hugging the south bank of the Big Black River and guarding the ferries against any attempted crossings by Pemberton's troops. With them rattled along several hundred wagons loaded with ammunition and a few staples like salt and coffee. They fought two minor preliminary battles with detachments from Pemberton's army and by the evening of May 13 had reached the vicinity of Jackson.

Vicksburg fell only after a siege of forty-seven days, much of it under shelling from Union gunboats and field artillery. Confederate civilians huddled in shelters like these. Cut off from the outside world, they were reduced, in some cases, to eating rats.

Ahead of them, a small Confederate force under General Joseph E. Johnston barred entrance to the city. The next day two Union corps attacked the rebels and pushed them north. In weeks to come Johnston would hover to the northeast of Grant's army, gather additional troops, and look for a way to help Pemberton defeat Grant. Grant never gave Johnston the opening.

After burning Jackson's war manufactories, the Union forces swung sharply west and headed for Vicksburg. Pemberton, meanwhile, moved east in search of Grant's nonexistent supply line. On May 16 elements of the two armies clashed at Champion's Hill, a commanding ridgeline about midway between Jackson and Vicksburg. Grant's troops managed to beat Pemberton and send his force in full retreat to the powerful Vicksburg fortifications. After a sharp action along the Big Black River with the Confederate rearguard, Grant's army reached the outskirts of the river city on May 18. There Grant resumed contact with Porter's gunboats, reestablished a solid line of supply, and began to invest the town.

Once Grant surrounded Vicksburg he made two quick tries to take the city by assault. The first attempt came on May 19, but the Confederates smashed it within minutes. A second, much more determined effort followed three days later. This time most of Grant's army rolled forward against the Confederate trenches that crowned the steep hillsides around Vicksburg, only to be stopped almost at once by a wall of musketry and artillery fire.

Grant suspended the attacks and settled down to a siege. In Washington, General-in-Chief Halleck funneled reinforcements to Grant's army as fast as possible. The Confederate government, meanwhile, met to consider how to avert impending disaster.

Gettysburg

The Confederate high command met in Richmond, weighed alternatives, and struggled to find a solution to the crisis. Secretary of War James Seddon favored dispatching reinforcements from Lee's army to help Pemberton throw Grant back. Then, with the threat to Vicksburg removed, Confederate forces could concentrate to help Bragg win decisively in central Tennessee. Davis agreed; so did James Longstreet, Lee's senior corps commander, although Longstreet reversed the priority: reinforcements should go first to Bragg, then Pemberton. Joe Johnston, P. G. T. Beauregard, and an informal network of other Confederate generals all concurred that some variation on this strategy should be attempted.

Lee, however, did not agree. Troops dispatched to succor Vicksburg, he said, could not reach the city in time to do anything if the fortress were in danger of imminent surrender. In Virginia, on the other hand, the Army of the Potomac could renew its advance at any time. Far from being in a position to donate troops to others, Lee insisted, "[U]nless we can obtain some reinforcements, we may be obliged to withdraw into the defences around Richmond."

The enormous prestige enjoyed by the South's greatest general compelled respect for his views. Davis called Lee to Richmond for a strategy conference on May 15. There, before the president and his assembled cabinet, Lee unveiled his own proposal. He would embark on an invasion of Pennsylvania. Such an offensive would remove the threat to Virginia and open the way to decisive victory on Union soil, with concurrent prospects for foreign recognition and a negotiated peace. At a minimum, he insisted, an invasion of the North would produce such consternation that the Federals would have to relax their grip on Vicksburg.

From anyone else, Lee's scheme would have seemed like the hallucination of an opium addict. But repeated success had given him the reputation of a miracle worker, and Davis saw Lee's point when the Virginian objected that the scheme to reinforce Vicksburg was highly problematic at best. "The answer of General Lee," he decided, "was such as I should have anticipated, and in which I concur."

Lee thus won permission to embark on his invasion of the North. Within three weeks his army was underway; by the end of June his troops had fanned out across southern Pennsylvania, where they courteously but thoroughly plundered the local population. In the meantime, Hooker brought the Army of the Potomac northward in pursuit.

By June 28 the Union army had entered Maryland, always keeping between Washington and Lee's forces. On that date, irritated by a rash of complaints from Hooker, Lincoln relieved him of command and replaced him with Major General George G. Meade, a well-respected but

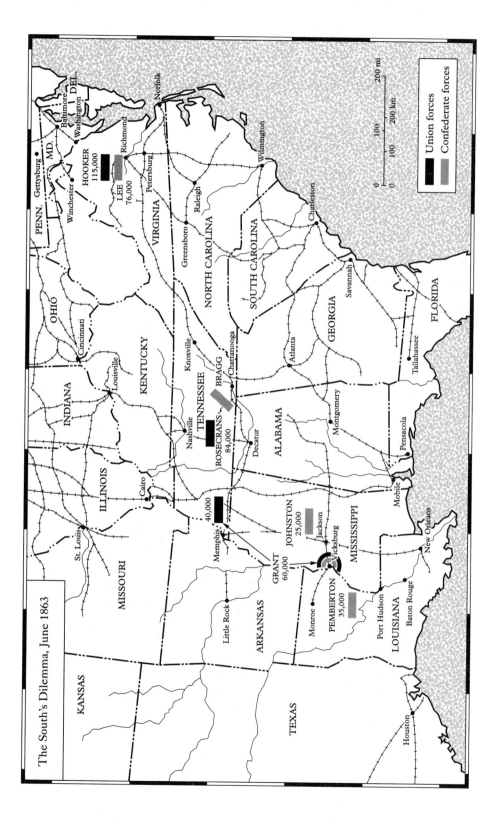

The South's Dilemma, June 1863

Union forces
Confederate forces

200 mi
100
0

200 km
100
0

PENN.
Gettysburg
MD.
Baltimore
Washington
DEL.
Winchester
Richmond
Norfolk
HOOKER
115,000
LEE
76,000
Petersburg
VIRGINIA
Raleigh
Greensboro
NORTH CAROLINA
Wilmington
SOUTH CAROLINA
Charleston

OHIO
Cincinnati
KENTUCKY
Louisville
INDIANA
Knoxville
Nashville
TENNESSEE
BRAGG
Chattanooga
ROSECRANS
84,000
Decatur
ALABAMA
Atlanta
GEORGIA
Montgomery
Savannah
Pensacola
Tallahassee
FLORIDA

ILLINOIS
Cairo
St. Louis
MISSOURI
Memphis
40,000
JOHNSTON
25,000
Jackson
Vicksburg
MISSISSIPPI
Mobile
New Orleans

GRANT
60,000
ARKANSAS
Little Rock
Monroe
PEMBERTON
35,000
Port Hudson
Baton Rouge
LOUISIANA

KANSAS
TEXAS
Houston

comparatively unknown corps commander. Meade thought it bad business to replace an army commander on the eve of battle and tried to decline; Lincoln, however, forced him to accept. Thus the Army of the Potomac approached its greatest battle with an untried leader at the helm.

Lee, meanwhile, did not realize that the Union army was so close to his own. Jeb Stuart—the "eyes" of the rebel army—had taken three brigades on a spectacular but pointless raid around the Union army and was far out of position. Not until June 30 did a spy inform Lee of the Union army's proximity. Lee promptly gave orders to reconcentrate his scattered divisions. The point chosen for the rendezvous was Gettysburg, a small town in south-central Pennsylvania, where a number of good roads converged.

On July 1 the first of Lee's troops approached Gettysburg. Elements of A. P. Hill's Confederate corps ran into Federal cavalry, which already occupied the town. Before long a sizable battle rocked and swelled amid the tidy farm lots north, west, and south of the town. Soon Union infantry came up. Both sides fed additional troops into the fight as soon as they arrived, but the Confederates had the advantage: their troops were closer and came onto the field more rapidly. A second Confederate corps under Lieutenant General Richard S. Ewell happened upon the Union right, north of Gettysburg, and pitched into it furiously. The Federal line cracked under the pressure. By late afternoon the Confederates had routed one corps, pummeled another, and driven the surviving Federals through Gettysburg. Hundreds of Northerners surrendered to closely pursuing rebels while the remaining Union troops withdrew south of the town to Cemetery Ridge.

Lee arrived on the field shortly after noon on July 1 but found the action so fluid and confused that he refrained from giving any orders. As daylight waned, however, he made two fateful decisions. First he elected to fight a general engagement around the fields and hills below Gettysburg, despite earlier doubts that his army was strong enough to fight a pitched battle against the larger Union army. Second, although he instructed Ewell to capture Cemetery Hill "if practicable," he failed to insist upon it. Ewell did not consider the move practicable and therefore did not attack. His reluctance to attack enabled the Federals to use Cemetery Hill, the northernmost point on Cemetery Ridge, as the foundation on which they constructed their entire defensive line.

During the night both sides received reinforcements as additional units took their places in the battle lines. The Union line south of Gettysburg began to take on its famous "fishhook" appearance: the barb at Culp's Hill southeast of the town, the curve at Cemetery Hill, and then a long shank that ran for a mile or so south along Cemetery Ridge. The Confederate II Corps faced Cemetery and Culp's hills while III Corps on its right faced Cemetery Ridge. Behind it lay I Corps under Lieutenant General James Longstreet. Recently arrived on the field and as yet unbloodied, I Corps would make the morrow's main attack. The target would be the Union left flank.

For the Confederates, the attack did not begin auspiciously—it was made without adequate reconnaissance and began only at 4:30 P.M. But the

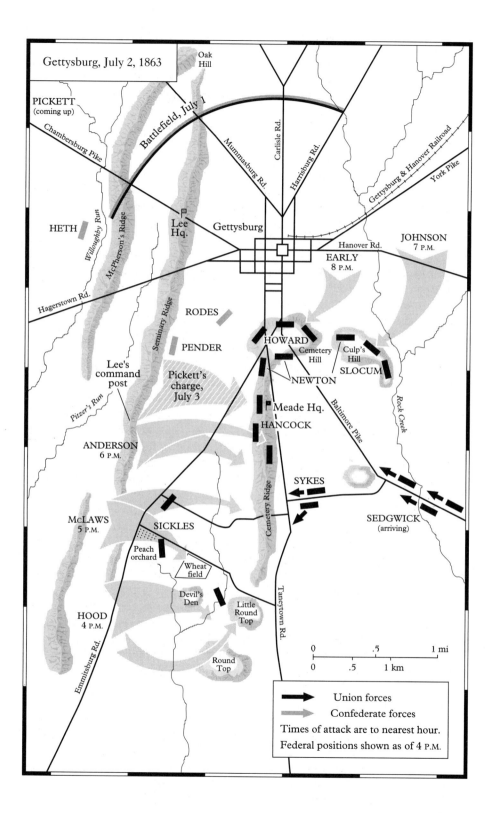

Gettysburg, July 2, 1863

PICKETT
(coming up)

Oak
Hill

Battlefield, July 1

Chambersburg Pike

Mummasburg Rd.

Carlisle Rd.

Harrisburg Rd.

Gettysburg & Hanover Railroad

York Pike

HETH

Willoughby Run

McPherson's Ridge

Lee
Hq.

Gettysburg

JOHNSON
7 P.M.

Hanover Rd.

EARLY
8 P.M.

Hagerstown Rd.

Seminary Ridge

RODES

PENDER

Lee's
command
post

Pitzer's Run

Pickett's
charge,
July 3

HOWARD

Cemetery
Hill

Culp's
Hill

SLOCUM

Rock Creek

NEWTON

Meade Hq.

HANCOCK

Baltimore Pike

ANDERSON
6 P.M.

Cemetery Ridge

SYKES

SEDGWICK
(arriving)

McLAWS
5 P.M.

SICKLES

Peach
orchard

Wheat
field

Taneytown Rd.

HOOD
4 P.M.

Devil's
Den

Little
Round
Top

Emmitsburg Rd.

Round
Top

0   .5   1 mi

0   .5   1 km

Union forces

Confederate forces

Times of attack are to nearest hour.
Federal positions shown as of 4 P.M.

blow fell like a thunderclap when it came. Afterward, Longstreet would call this attack "the best two hours' fighting done by any troops on any battlefield." It certainly showed both armies at the height of their powers. As such, the engagement well illustrates the dynamics of a Civil War battle.

Longstreet's attack began with massed artillery fire. The cannoneers fired solid shot to disable enemy batteries and shell to strike his foot soldiers. The artillery was still firing when the rebel infantry advanced: two divisions from Longstreet's own corps, supported by a third from another corps. The divisions advanced *en echelon*—that is, one after another, from the right end of the line toward the left—a tactic designed to mislead the enemy as to the actual focus of the assault. The infantry regiments marched steadily, trying hard to maintain their two-line, shoulder-to-shoulder battle formation despite the hilly, wooded terrain. Brigade and regimental commanders supervised their units closely. Their main duty was to preserve the troops' linear formation and to prevent their units from crossing in front of one another or spreading out too far.

In severe fighting the Confederates smashed a badly positioned Union corps and plunged up the steep, rocky slopes of Little Round Top, a hill at the end of the Union left flank. Last-minute reinforcements beat back the Confederates there and restored the front; particularly memorable was the famous defense by the 20th Maine Regiment under Colonel Joshua Lawrence Chamberlain. But the fighting swirled back and forth until nightfall. Amid the deafening noise of musketry and cannon fire, each side struggled to secure local superiority at several key points. For the commanders the job was mainly to "feed the fight"—finding and throwing in whatever reinforcements became available—while encouraging their soldiers and rallying them when a short retreat became necessary. For the individual soldiers, the job was to maintain "touch of elbows" with the man on either side, follow the regimental colors—in the smoke and din the movement of these flags often became a primary means of communication—and fire low. Despite the greatly increased range of the rifled musket, this engagement, like many Civil War battles, was actually fought well within smoothbore range. The two sides were often only a few dozen yards apart. Sometimes they collided; when they did, a desperate close-quarters struggle with clubbed muskets and even bare fists would result.

Several times Longstreet's men came close to victory. But ultimately the combination of rough terrain and tough Union resistance exhausted them, and the attack fell short of success. Things were no better on the battlefield's opposite end. Ewell failed to begin a secondary attack until dusk and won little but casualties for his pains. The Union position had proven too strong, the Confederate thrusts too late or too weak.

Lee remained determined to continue the offensive. The great stubbornness that had displayed itself at the Seven Days, Antietam, and Chancellorsville seemed more entrenched than ever at Gettysburg. Despite the failures on July 2, Lee perceived amid the reports glimmerings of potential success: good artillery positions *had* been seized, charging divisions had *almost* broken through, probing brigades had come *close* to breaching the Union center. Then reinforcements arrived in the form of Stuart's long-lost

The recently invented technique of photography captured the grisly aftermath of Civil War battles. Nearly 620,000 Americans died in the Civil War, far more than in any other conflict.

cavalry and an infantry division under Major General George Pickett. Morale remained good, and Southern valor could still be counted upon. Lee ordered Longstreet to renew the attack the next day.

Longstreet, however, opposed the plan and urged that the Confederate army try an envelopment or a turning movement instead. Lee listened courteously, then instructed Longstreet to attack the Union center with three divisions spearheaded by Pickett's men. After a long preliminary bombardment by Confederate artillery, the climactic attack began on the afternoon of July 3. Fifteen thousand rebel soldiers in battle lines that stretched nearly a mile from flank to flank surged from the wooded crest of Seminary Ridge and headed toward a clump of trees that marked the center of the Union line. The gallant men in whom Lee vested such outsized confidence charged bravely and died bravely but never had a chance. Napoleonic assaults of that sort could no longer win against veteran troops firing rifles that could kill at ranges of 300 yards or more. Nor could they prevail against canister—artillery rounds made up of lead slugs that transformed cannon into huge sawed-off shotguns. Valor was not at issue, for as a general who helped lead the charge claimed, "If the troops I commanded could not take that position, all Hell couldn't take it." What lay at issue were the tactical realities of 1863. By that time, the balance of strength had tilted sharply from the offensive to the defensive.

Pickett's charge illustrated both the lethal effectiveness of artillery on the defensive and a corresponding weakness on the offensive. Although Union cannon scythed down the Confederate attackers in droves, the preliminary Confederate artillery bombardment, although massive and intense, signally failed to create the conditions for a successful infantry assault. In the days of Napoleon, artillery batteries might have advanced to a point just outside smoothbore musket range and battered down the enemy infantry line, but the extended range of the rifled musket—coupled with effective counterbattery fire from the new rifled artillery—made such a tactic impossible. Some Confederate batteries did, in fact, move forward in support of Pickett's attack but nowhere near as far as their Napoleonic counterparts might have gone.

The survivors of what became known as "Pickett's Charge" came streaming back across the field, leaving their dead and dying comrades strewn across the shallow valley that separated the rival positions. Lee rode among the returning troops, shaken, saddened, and moved to a strange, almost wistful tenderness. "It's all my fault," he would tell Longstreet later. "I thought my men were invincible."

Lee lost nearly 20,000 men at Gettysburg. During the retreat he nearly lost his entire army. Summer storms caused the Potomac to rise, barring passage to the retreating Confederate forces. With the fords unusable and the bridges long since destroyed, the beaten Confederates faced annihilation if Meade's Federals caught up with them and launched a determined assault. Meade, however, pursued cautiously. Minor skirmishing ensued, but no major attack. While a jury-rigged ferryboat shipped handfuls of men across, Lee's engineers built a pontoon bridge—a crazy patchwork of planks, scows, and barges completed on July 13. The wagons crept across it, and the infantry waded to safety through chest-high water. The Army of Northern Virginia was saved, scarcely twenty-four hours before Meade planned to launch a belated attack.

Captured during Lee's retreat from Pennsylvania, three rebel soldiers await transportation to a Union prison camp. The Confederate defeats at Gettysburg and Vicksburg occurred within a day of each other and together marked the war's military turning point.

Lincoln was disappointed. He thought Meade had blown a spectacular chance to wreck Lee's army for good. But Meade had probably done as well as was possible. For one thing, at Gettysburg his army had suffered tremendous casualties of its own. For another, the Confederate bridgehead on the Potomac was heavily fortified; an attack against it would most likely have failed. Most important, Meade's successful defense at Gettysburg had inflicted 33 percent casualties on Lee's army and, as it turned out, blunted forever its offensive capability. And coupled with Grant's victory at Vicksburg, Gettysburg offered important new proof that the North was winning the war.

Vicksburg fell on July 4, 1863, after a siege of nearly seven weeks. Inside the town food had grown desperately short; toward the end of the siege, soldiers and civilians started eating horsemeat and rats. Outside, Grant's army bided its time, dined comfortably on the plentitude of supplies arriving at their new river base, and grew steadily stronger as additional troops reinforced those already on the scene. (Grant had conducted his May offensive with about 44,000 men; by the end of the siege he had over 70,000 men in all.)

The capture of Vicksburg reopened the Mississippi River and severed Arkansas, Texas, and much of Louisiana from the rest of the Confederacy, but these results were largely symbolic. The midwestern states had learned to ship their goods by rail, and they continued to do so even after the "Father of Waters" again became an available conduit. The real significance lay in the capture of Pemberton's entire army—nearly 31,000 Confederate troops became prisoners, together with 172 cannon and about 60,000 small arms. The Confederacy could scarcely afford such losses.

Struggle for the Gateway

While Grant was besieging Vicksburg and Lee was advancing and retreating in the East, a third campaign, more prolonged than either of the other two, was underway along the southern fringe of the Appalachian highlands. From June until November 1863 Union and Confederate armies grappled for possession of Chattanooga, a strategic railroad city in southeastern Tennessee. In addition to its significance as the place where three major railroads met, Chattanooga also formed the principal gateway into Unionist Tennessee, whose occupation had been a cherished objective of the Lincoln administration since the war's outset. Even more important, it was the northern end of a corridor that led a hundred miles south to Atlanta, Georgia.

In a real sense, the capture of Chattanooga was more important than that of Vicksburg. With the seizure of the latter city, the Mississippi River was reopened and the strategic purpose of a thrust in that direction reached its logical culmination. But Chattanooga was not only a major objective in its own right; it opened the way to further attacks into the Southern

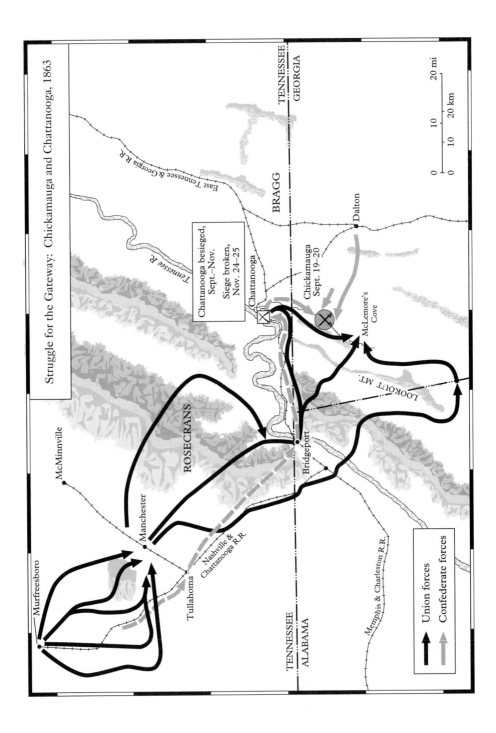

Struggle for the Gateway: Chickamauga and Chattanooga, 1863

McMinnville

Murfreesboro

Manchester

Tullahoma

Nashville & Chattanooga R.R.

ROSECRANS

Bridgeport

Memphis & Charleston R.R.

TENNESSEE
ALABAMA

Tennessee R.

East Tennessee & Georgia R.R.

Chattanooga

Chattanooga besieged,
Sept.–Nov.

Siege broken,
Nov. 24–25

Chickamauga
Sept. 19–20

McLemore's
Cove

LOOKOUT MT.

BRAGG

Dalton

TENNESSEE
GEORGIA

Union forces
Confederate forces

0   10   20 mi

0   10   20 km

heartland. As events developed, the most fatal blows to the Confederacy would originate from this modest town, hugging a bend in the Tennessee River in the massive shadow of Lookout Mountain. Small wonder that for five months, well over 150,000 men struggled for possession of this city, a struggle in which some 47,000 of them became casualties.

Prologue to Chickamauga

The drive toward Chattanooga did not begin until the year 1863 was almost half over. After the bloody stalemate at Stone's River around New Year's Day, 1863, both the Army of the Cumberland and the Army of Tennessee entered a long period of quiet recuperation. Bragg lacked the numbers to undertake an active campaign. Rosecrans, despite much cajoling from his superiors in Washington, stubbornly refused to begin an advance until he was certain that his army was ready for a sustained offensive that promised decisive results. His subordinates agreed. "We certainly cannot fight the enemy for the mere purpose of whipping him," wrote a division commander. "The time has passed when the fate of armies must be staked because the newspapers have no excitement and do not sell well. I think our people have now comprehended that a battle is a very grave thing."

This was particularly the case if the battle under consideration promised to do no more than push the enemy back a few dozen miles, which was all the carnage at Stone's River the previous winter had done. Instead, Rosecrans hoped that an adroit campaign of maneuver could compel Bragg to fall back all the way to Chattanooga without major fighting. The climactic struggle, when it came, would then be fought for possession of the city itself. Such a thrust, however—effective *and* bloodless—required Rosecrans to place his entire army in Bragg's rear while maintaining his own communications intact. It was one of the most difficult maneuvers in warfare; no Civil War general had managed the feat (although at Second Manassas Lee had come close).

Rosecrans, then, was playing for very high stakes. To win, he believed, required two things. First he must not advance before he was ready. Second, the advance, when made, must be swift and unswerving. It turned out that Rosecrans had a very exacting idea of what it meant to be ready. Not until June 23 did he believe he possessed sufficient cavalry and supply reserves to advance. But when he did he conducted one of the Civil War's most remarkable campaigns. In little more than two weeks of hard marching—punctuated by minor skirmishes in which his army lost just 560 men—Rosecrans seized a key gap in the Cumberland Plateau, turned Bragg's right flank, and forced him to retreat all the way to Chattanooga, a distance of eighty miles. The rough terrain and great difficulty in supplying his army then compelled a pause of several weeks while Rosecrans consolidated his gains. In August he resumed the advance, this time turning Bragg's left flank. While Union artillery kept up a brisk demonstration against Chattanooga, distracting Bragg's attention in that direction, a Union infantry corps crossed the Tennessee River below the town. With his communications now in imminent jeopardy, Bragg abandoned Chattanooga.

The strategic railway city and gateway to the Confederate heartland fell without a fight on September 9.

Predictably, the loss of Chattanooga spurred the Confederate high command to dramatic action. Even before Rosecrans had resumed his advance in August, President Jefferson Davis had considered the possibility of strongly reinforcing Bragg with troops drawn from Joe Johnston in Mississippi. Subsequently Davis conducted a series of conferences with Lee over a two-week period, at the end of which Lee agreed to detach two divisions from his Army of Northern Virginia. These divisions would go by railroad to support Bragg's army; then, with luck and skill, the Army of Tennessee might destroy Rosecrans's force, retrieve Chattanooga, and possibly advance into middle Tennessee.

The most direct line, the Virginia and Tennessee Railroad, was unavailable because of the recent loss of Knoxville, and the two divisions were forced to travel by a circuitous route that doubled the beeline distance. Led by James Longstreet, the reinforcing Confederates rattled along no fewer than ten railroads on dilapidated cars, with frequent transfers and attendant delays. They left Lee's army on September 9, the same day that Chattanooga fell. It took ten days for the first troops to reach Bragg's army. Two-thirds made it in time for the battle then brewing. With their assistance, the Army of Tennessee won its greatest victory.

Chickamauga

The apparent ease with which he had shoved Bragg out of middle Tennessee and Chattanooga made Rosecrans overconfident. Although inordinately careful in his preparations, once on the march Rosecrans tended to be aggressive. As Rosecrans's Union troops swung into northern Georgia in early September, he believed Bragg's Confederates were demoralized and on the defensive. In his judgment, it was important to keep up the pressure and give his opponent no opportunity to sort things out. Bragg, however, was hardly demoralized. Secure in the knowledge that he was about to be reinforced, the Confederate commander kept looking for chances to strike the Federal invaders a resounding blow.

The mountainous Georgia countryside gave Bragg several opportunities, for it forced Rosecrans to send his columns through widely separated gaps. On two occasions the Union commander inadvertently gave the Confederates an excellent chance to concentrate against one or another exposed segment of his army, but on each occasion Bragg's subordinates botched the opportunity. Finally alert to the danger his army was in, Rosecrans ordered his scattered units to concentrate near West Chickamauga Creek about twelve miles south of Chattanooga.

On September 19, Bragg attacked. The two-day battle that ensued was fought in a dense tangle of second-growth timber broken at intervals by small open fields. Both sides had difficulty effectively controlling their units in such terrain; the engagement was really more a series of individual firefights than one concerted battle. The Confederates, for once, had the edge in manpower: about 66,000 rebel effectives against roughly 56,000 Federals. But in the first day's fighting this advantage was largely nullified by Bragg's faulty grasp of the Union dispositions and the confused nature of the fighting, which led to his troops being committed piecemeal. Late in the evening, however, he reorganized his army into two informal wings, placed them under his senior commanders—Lieutenant Generals Longstreet and Leonidas Polk—and made plans to resume the battle next morning.

The fighting on September 20 began about 9:30 A.M. and consisted of a series of sequential attacks made from north to south. None of these charges made much headway, however, and by 11 A.M. Bragg abandoned this *en echelon* approach in favor of a straightforward thrust by his remaining force. Until this moment the Federals had waged a capable defense and by and large had rebuffed every Confederate attack. In the process, however, Rosecrans was forced to shift some of his units from one threatened point to another—much as Lee had done at Antietam. But where Lee had conducted this delicate operation almost flawlessly, Rosecrans—in part confused by the terrain—made a major mistake. Seeking to plug a small hole in his line, he ordered a division shifted from one part of the field to another. That, in turn, created a very large hole: a hole, it turned out, just where four divisions under Longstreet were moving to attack.

The result, of course, was a shattering defeat for the Union army as some 20,000 Confederates poured into the gap. Three entire Union divisions ceased to exist as organized units; two more divisions had to withdraw from the field and could not return to the fray until evening. Rosecrans himself, crestfallen and dispirited, virtually abandoned the field. Two of his corps commanders did the same. Only a magnificent stand by a Union corps under Major General George H. Thomas saved Rosecrans's army from complete disaster. In a masterful defense of Snodgrass Hill in the center of the battlefield, Thomas blunted the momentum of the Confederate attack and enabled the rest of the army to withdraw intact. For that achievement he was known ever after as the "Rock of Chickamauga."

Confederate casualties in the battle totaled 18,454; the Union lost 16,170. Rosecrans's army fell back exhausted into Chattanooga. Bragg refused to pursue vigorously and elected to besiege the Union army by holding the high ground south and east of the town. Despite the victory, most of his subordinates were disgruntled with Bragg's battlefield performance and the way in which he tamely let Rosecrans escape enraged at least one of them. "What does he fight battles for?" growled Confederate cavalry leader Nathan Bedford Forrest. Still, the Army of the Cumberland had suffered a signal defeat, and if it were starved into surrender at Chattanooga, the Union disaster would undo most of what the victories at Vicksburg and Gettysburg had achieved.

Missionary Ridge

In this crisis the Lincoln administration turned to Grant. At the end of September, Secretary of War Edwin M. Stanton arranged an emergency conference with Grant at Louisville, Kentucky. There he gave Grant an order placing him in charge of substantially the entire western theater— everything from the Mississippi River to the Appalachian Mountains except Louisiana. Stanton also asked Grant to decide whether Rosecrans should be relieved. Grant thought he should, and Rosecrans was replaced by Major General George H. Thomas.

The Lincoln administration took one other decisive step as well. It withdrew two entire corps—20,000 men—from Meade's Army of the Potomac and sent them west to reinforce the beleaguered troops in Chattanooga. Railroads had been used throughout the conflict to shuttle troops about, but this September 1863 movement was a logistical tour de force. Within forty hours of the initial decision, the first units were on their way west. Eleven days and 1,200 miles later practically all the detached troops, together with their artillery, horses, and wagons, had reached Bridgeport, Alabama, staging point for the relief of Chattanooga.

Late in October, Grant personally went to Chattanooga to have a closer look at the situation. His party rode on horseback via the only route that remained open into or out of the city—a narrow road, hardly more than a bridle path in spots, that wound about sixty-five miles from Bridgeport to Chattanooga through a desolate stretch of mountains. This road formed the only means by which the besieged Army of the Cumberland could receive supplies. The supplies amounted to hardly more than a trickle, and once at Chattanooga Grant discovered that the horses were starving and the men not far from it.

Efforts to repair the situation got under way as soon as Grant arrived. Within days the Union troops broke out of their encirclement enough to reestablish a solid supply line through the Tennessee River valley—a "Cracker Line," the men called it. Along with a welcome deluge of rations, thousands of reinforcements arrived to help drive away the Confederate army. In addition to the two corps from Virginia, most of Grant's own Army of the Tennessee, now led by red-bearded General Sherman, came up from Mississippi. A new spirit entered the beleaguered army at Chattanooga. "You have no conception of the change in the army when Grant came," one soldier testified. "He opened up the cracker line and got a steamer through. We began to see things move. We felt that everything came from a plan. He came into the army quietly, no splendor, no airs, no staff. He used to go about alone. He began the campaign the moment he reached the field."

By mid-autumn the Union armies were ready to attack, and on November 24–25 they conducted a series of offensives aimed at breaking the Confederate grip on Chattanooga. The unexpected climax of these battles occurred on the second day of fighting, when Thomas's Army of the Cumberland transformed what had been planned as a limited thrust into a wild, hell-for-leather charge up the rugged slopes of Missionary Ridge, smack into the center of the whole Confederate line. It seemed impossible that such a charge could succeed, and Grant, watching the impromptu attack, remarked that if it failed whoever had ordered the assault was going to sweat for it. Yet, incredibly, the Union troops made it to the top and routed the astonished Confederates.

At first glance the victory appeared, if not a "visible interposition of God," as someone remarked, then at least a vindication of continued faith in the frontal assault. In fact it could more accurately be seen as the harvest of sloppy Confederate planning. Most of the Confederate defenders had been placed, not at the military crest of the ridge—the highest point from which a marksman could hit what was below him—but at the topographical crest, where he generally could not hit much of anything. In addition, a good number of rebel soldiers had been deployed at the foot of the ridge, where they were too few to stop the Federal advance, but sufficiently numerous, when they retreated, to force their comrades at the summit to hold their fire. Finally, the Confederates had neglected to cover the numerous ravines that led to the top, so that the assaulting Federal columns found numerous covered avenues as they scrambled up the slope.

Thus through Bragg's failure to pursue Rosecrans after Chickamauga and his mismanaged siege of Chattanooga, the Federals were able to restore the situation, secure permanent control of this gateway city, and win a glittering autumn victory at surprisingly low cost. The Union lost 5,800 men, slightly more than 10 percent of the total engaged. The Confederates lost 6,700 out of 46,000, and embarked on a retreat that did not end until they reached Dalton, Georgia, some twenty-five miles away. The road into the Southern heartland was now open.

Even after the North decided to recruit African Americans as soldiers, fears persisted that blacks would not make effective soldiers. As units like the 54th Massachusetts demonstrated, such fears were misplaced. Its assault at Fort Wagner, South Carolina, in July 1863 was one of the most famous of the war.

* * * *

By the end of 1863 the Confederacy had lost not only two key strategic points—Vicksburg and Chattanooga—it had also lost a great deal of its ability to counterpunch effectively. Lee's great victory at Chancellorsville and his great disaster at Gettysburg had, between them, cost the South about 33,000 men. Roughly the same number went into the bag with Pemberton's capitulation at Vicksburg. The Confederacy simply could not afford to sustain such casualties. It had nearly reached the bottom of its manpower pool, and the losses of 1863 included many of its most experienced and motivated soldiers. The North, by contrast, still had ample manpower reserves. It also had begun to reap one advantage of the Emancipation Proclamation by recruiting and fielding thousands of African-American troops. The first black units had their baptism of fire in 1863 and, to the surprise of white men North and South, performed with courage and élan. Ultimately a full 10 percent of the Union army—180,000 men in all—would be composed of black soldiers.

The reversals of 1863 also began a long-term decline in Confederate morale. The South had endured at least one previous crisis of confidence, during the first six months of 1862, but this second crisis was just as bad. Desertions swelled in the months after Gettysburg and Vicksburg as soldiers decided that "we are done gon up the Spout." A Confederate war department clerk described Chattanooga as an "incalculable disaster," while the wife of a prominent Southern leader wrote that "gloom and unspoken despondency hang like a pall everywhere." As the New Year approached, Southerners knew that the most terrible trial of the war was at hand.

SUGGESTED READINGS

Black, Robert C., III. *The Railroads of the Confederacy* (Chapel Hill: University of North Carolina Press, 1952).

Catton, Bruce. *Grant Moves South* (Boston: Little, Brown, 1960).

———. *Never Call Retreat* (Garden City, N.Y.: Doubleday, 1965).

Coddington, Edwin A. *The Gettysburg Campaign: A Study in Command* (New York: Charles Scribner's Sons, 1968).

Connelly, Thomas L. *Autumn of Glory: The Army of Tennessee, 1863–1865* (Baton Rouge: Louisiana State University Press, 1970).

Cornish, Dudley Taylor. *The Sable Arm: Black Troops in the Union Army, 1861–1865* (New York: Longmans, Green, 1956).

Cozzens, Peter. *This Terrible Sound: The Battle of Chickamauga* (Urbana and Chicago: University of Illinois Press, 1992).

Escott, Paul D. *After Secession: Jefferson Davis and the Failure of Confederate Nationalism* (Baton Rouge: Louisiana State University Press, 1979).

Furgurson, Ernest B. *Chancellorsville 1863: The Souls of the Brave* (New York: Alfred A. Knopf, 1992).

Geary, John. *We Need Men: The Union Draft in the Civil War, 1861–1865* (DeKalb: Northern Illinois University Press, 1990).

Glatthaar, Joseph T. *Forged in Battle: The Civil War Alliance of Black Soldiers and White Officers* (New York: Free Press, 1989).

Griffith, Paddy. *Civil War Battle Tactics* (New Haven, Conn.: Yale University Press, 1989).

Hagerman, Edward. *The American Civil War and the Origins of Modern Warfare* (Bloomington: Indiana University Press, 1988).

McWhiney, Grady, and Perry D. Jamieson. *Attack and Die: Civil War Military Tactics and the Southern Heritage* (University, Ala.: University of Alabama Press, 1982).

Paludan, Philip S. *A People's Contest: The Union and the Civil War, 1861–1865* (New York: Harper & Row, 1988).

Royster, Charles. *The Destructive War: William Tecumseh Sherman, Stonewall Jackson, and the Americans* (New York: Alfred A. Knopf, 1991).

Weber, Thomas. *The Northern Railroads in the Civil War, 1861–1865* (Westport, Conn.: Greenwood Press, 1952).

5

THE CIVIL WAR, 1864–1865:
TOTAL WAR

The Virginia Campaign

To Atlanta and Beyond

The Naval War, 1862–1865

The War Ends

The final year of the Civil War witnessed the full bloom of total war. No western state in centuries had waged a military contest more comprehensively than did the Union and Confederacy. Determined national efforts the world had seen: during the Napoleonic Wars the Spanish and Russian people had fought relentlessly against the French invaders; and in 1813 the Russians had pursued the retreating French for nearly a thousand miles. Yet neither the Spanish nor the Russians had mobilized their populations and economies as systematically as did the North and South. Also, when the allies carried the war into France in 1814, they did not make a sustained effort to destroy the French people's capacity to make war. By 1864, however, the North was not only bringing pressure against the Confederate field armies but was also striking powerfully at the material and psychological resources of the South.

In strictly military terms, the South now had little chance to win the war. With Lee's offensive power blunted, the trans-Mississippi isolated, and Chattanooga in Union hands, the Confederacy's strategic situation was bleak. Moreover, the battles of previous years had bled rebel manpower so heavily that by early 1864 the Confederate Congress was forced to pass a new conscription law that abolished substitutes and "robbed the cradle and the grave" in an effort to secure more troops. Even this did not help. In desperation, a few Confederate leaders began to ponder the previously unthinkable option of using slaves as soldiers—and, in exchange, to emancipate those slaves who agreed to fight for the South.

Most, however, continued to regard this last step as anathema. Instead they pinned their hopes on the fact that in November 1864, Lincoln faced reelection. If the South could only hold out until then, the war weariness of Northerners might result in his losing the White House. "If we can break up the enemy's arrangements early, and throw him back," noted one Confederate general, "he will not be able to recover his position or his morale until the Presidential election is over, and then we shall have a new President to treat with." Presumably this new president would be receptive to a compromise peace.

Lincoln, of course, understood the rebel hope as well as anyone, and he had no intention of permitting a prolonged stalemate. Instead he did what most observers had assumed he would do since the triumph at Chattanooga: he gave Ulysses S. Grant command of all the Union armies. With the new job came the three stars of a lieutenant general, a rank not held by any U.S. officer (except honorifically) since George Washington. In March 1864, Grant came to Washington, met Lincoln for the first time, received his promotion, and settled down to win the war.

The Virginia Campaign

Now installed as general-in-chief (with Halleck retained as army chief of staff), Grant began planning at once for the 1864 campaigns. The content of those plans and the way in which he devised them provide a good lens through which to examine the salient features of his generalship.

To begin with, Grant saw the war as a whole. Until that time most Union generals had viewed the conflict in terms of separate theaters; no one placed much premium on cooperative effort. As a result, the outnumbered Confederate forces had been able to shift troops from one place to another, shoring up one threatened point by diverting strength from quiet sectors. In this way Johnston had gathered over 30,000 soldiers for his vain but bothersome effort to relieve Vicksburg; in this way as well, troops from all over the Confederacy had gathered to administer the near-crippling blow to Rosecrans at Chickamauga. To prevent the Confederates from shifting troops from quiet to threatened sectors, Grant planned for a simultaneous advance along the entire front.

Second, Grant was less interested in occupying "strategic points" than in destroying the enemy's main forces. He believed that when no armies remained to defend them, the strategic points would fall as a matter of course. Important cities like Richmond and Atlanta were useful chiefly because the main Confederate armies would fight for them, and in the course of fighting they could be destroyed. Grant put this concept succinctly in a letter to Major General George Gordon Meade, commander of the Army of the Potomac: "Lee's army is your objective point. Wherever Lee goes, there you will go also."

Third, Grant wanted the 1864 spring offensive to be as strong as possible. He regretted the detachment of so many Union troops on passive occupation duty. Some of this could not be helped—by this period of the

The architect of victory. Appointed to command the Union armies in March 1864, Ulysses S. Grant quickly applied a strategy of maintaining constant military pressure on the Confederacy through coordinated offensives to wear down Southern armies and destroy Southern war resources.

war the Federal armies had to contend with well over 100,000 square miles of captured hostile territory—but it struck Grant that all too often the passive stance was unnecessary. At an April conference with Lincoln, Grant expressed the view that these detachments could do their jobs "just as well by advancing as by remaining still; and by advancing they would compel the enemy to keep detachments to hold them back, or else lay his own territory open to invasion." Lincoln grasped the point at once. "Oh, yes!" he said. "I see that. As we say out West, if a man can't skin he must hold a leg while somebody else does."

Finally, Grant expected to combine destruction of Southern armies with destruction of Southern war resources. Although Sherman would become the general most identified with this policy, Grant had a profound understanding of the fact that Civil War armies had become too large and too powerful to destroy in battle. Their annihilation required not only military defeat but also the elimination of the foodstuffs, forage, ammunition, and equipage necessary to maintain them in the field. His instructions to Sherman reflect this: "You I propose to move against [Joseph E.] Johnston's army, to break it up, and to get into the interior of the enemy's country as far as you can, inflicting all the damage you can against their war resources."

Grant refused to direct operations from Washington and decided to make his headquarters with the Army of the Potomac. He had good reason

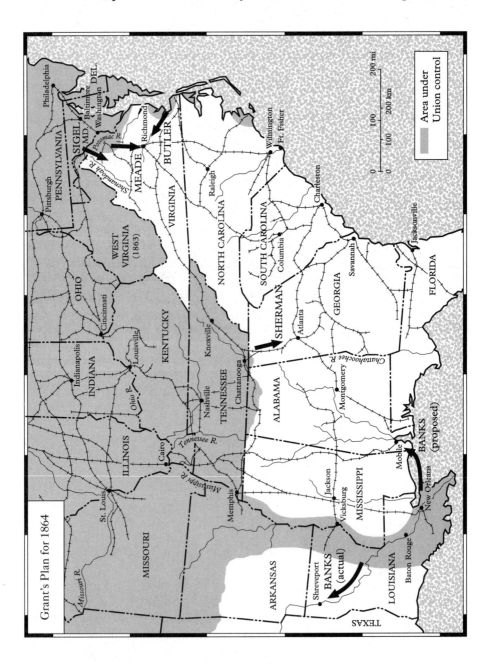

Grant's Plan for 1864

for doing so. That army formed one of the two primary concentrations of Union force; as such it would play a decisive role in the campaign to come. But except for its single defensive victory at Gettysburg, the Army of the Potomac had a depressing record of stalemate or defeat; in its entire existence it had never won a clear-cut offensive victory. Worse, the army had traditionally suffered from its close proximity to Washington, which made it strongly susceptible to political pressures and even to factionalism among the officer corps. In short, the Army of the Potomac seemed to need first-hand attention far more than the other reservoir of Federal striking power—the combined armies of the Cumberland, the Tennessee, and the Ohio—which Sherman had assembled at Chattanooga. Sherman, in any event, enjoyed Grant's entire confidence.

Grant also came to think highly of General Meade, leader of the Army of the Potomac. He had never met Meade before his arrival in Virginia and did not know what to expect, but Meade impressed him by offering to step aside immediately if Grant wished to put someone in his place. Grant declined the offer and Meade remained in command; even so, Grant exerted such close supervision over the Army of the Potomac that it quickly became known, erroneously but enduringly, as "Grant's army."

Grant's final plan for the great 1864 campaign pressed the Confederacy on all sides: in the eastern theater, the Army of the Potomac would advance against General Robert E. Lee's Army of Northern Virginia. Two smaller forces would "hold a leg": Major General Franz Sigel would advance up the Shenandoah Valley while Major General Benjamin F. Butler would conduct an amphibious operation against the Richmond-Petersburg area. Unfortunately, Sigel and Butler were political generals, men of little or no military ability who held important commands exclusively because they had strong influence with constituencies important to the Union war effort. (Sigel was a hero among the German-American community, Butler an important Democrat.) Grant would have been justified in expecting nothing at all from these men. Instead he pinned many of his hopes for the upcoming Virginia campaign on the belief that both would perform capably. Grant gave Butler an especially significant role: he anticipated that Butler's army would be able to seize the important railroad town of Petersburg and perhaps even capture Richmond itself.

Out west, Sherman's three armies would move upon Johnston's Army of Tennessee. Grant had hoped that yet another force, under General Banks, might advance from Louisiana against Mobile, Alabama, but for political reasons Banks marched up the cotton-rich but strategically irrelevant Red River valley. Except for Banks, who had already made—and lost—his campaign by early April, the remaining operations were timed to jump off simultaneously in early May 1864.

The Wilderness and Spotsylvania

Grant, of course, paid closest attention to the offensive against Lee. On May 4 the Army of the Potomac crossed the Rapidan River into the

Wilderness, the same region where Hooker had come to grief the year before. Some miles to the west lay Lee's Army of Northern Virginia. By crossing here, Grant hoped to turn Lee's right flank and compel him to retreat. But that same day Lee got his troops in motion and came thundering east; early the next morning he hurled them into action against two Union corps as they struggled along the narrow lanes of the Wilderness.

Outnumbered nearly two to one (64,000 men against Grant's 119,000), Lee wanted to force a battle in the Wilderness where thick woods would dilute the Union numerical advantage and make it difficult for the Federals to use their numerous and well-trained artillery. During the next two days he savaged the Union army with a sustained intensity Grant had never experienced in his previous campaigns. Those who *had* experienced it were not slow to offer advice. On the second day of the fighting one Union general told him, "General Grant, this is a crisis that cannot be looked upon too seriously. I know Lee's methods well by past experience; he will throw his whole army between us and the Rapidan, and cut us off completely from our communications." Usually phlegmatic, Grant permitted himself a rare show of annoyance. "Oh, I am heartily tired of hearing what Lee is going to do. Some of you always seem to think he is suddenly going to turn a double somersault and land in our rear and on both of our flanks at the same time. Go back to your command," he snapped, "and try to think what we are going to do ourselves, instead of what Lee is going to do."

This kind of thinking brought something new to the Army of the Potomac. The fighting in the Wilderness cost the Union nearly 17,000 casu-

In Virginia, Grant's 1864 campaign began with two bitter days of fighting in the densely wooded Wilderness. Many wounded men on both sides were burned to death when the trees and undergrowth caught fire. Despite harrowing losses, Grant maintained pressure on Lee's army.

alties; Lee, by contrast suffered no more than about 10,000. In earlier days the Army of the Potomac would have retreated after such a battle to lick its wounds. Grant, however, decided simply to disengage and continue his effort to get around Lee's flank. After suffering for years from a chronic sense of inferiority, the Army of the Potomac found itself led by a man who never thought in terms of defeat and who did not lose his will to fight when confronted by casualties.

The army began moving during the evening of May 7, heading for Spotsylvania Court House, an important crossroads, ten miles southeast of the Wilderness, whose swift possession would allow the Union forces to interpose between Richmond and Lee. Confederate troops got there first, however, and in a series of sharp little engagements held the crossroads long enough for Lee's army to arrive in strength. For twelve days (May 9–21), the two armies grappled inconclusively in the fields north and east of Spotsylvania.

Unlike the Wilderness, where Lee had counterattacked early and often, at Spotsylvania the Army of Northern Virginia fought almost entirely behind entrenchments. Grant viewed this as a confession of Confederate weakness. At the same time, however, he found it very difficult to crack the rebel line. On May 10, for example, an imaginative young West Point graduate named Emory Upton managed to break into the Confederate entrenchments using a new tactical scheme of his own devising. His division advanced in column formation, without pausing to fire en route—Upton took the precaution of having his men charge with muskets uncapped except for the leading rank. The attack indeed broke the rebel line, but supporting Federal troops failed to arrive and Upton reluctantly withdrew.

Grant, however, was sufficiently impressed with the new tactic to try it again, this time using an entire corps. Shortly after dawn on May 12 the corps struck a prominent salient in the Confederate position known as the "Mule Shoe." As in Upton's charge, the Federals broke through the enemy trenches, this time capturing more than 4,000 prisoners. Lee was forced to counterattack in a desperate attempt to restore the breach, resulting in some of the most ferocious combat of the entire war. In many places the fighting was hand to hand, and at one point the bullets flew so thick that an oak tree nearly two feet in diameter was completely cut in two. By evening Lee managed to complete a new line of entrenchments across the base of the Mule Shoe, and the surviving Confederates withdrew. In a pattern that would be repeated endlessly during World War I, the defenders had managed to repair a breach in their fortified line faster than the attackers could exploit it.

To the Banks of the James River

Initially Grant was determined to break the Confederates at Spotsylvania—he wired Washington, "I propose to fight it out on this line if it takes all summer." But by mid-May it had become obvious that both secondary offensives in Virginia had failed. A hastily assembled rebel force defeated Sigel on May 15 at the Battle of New Market. Butler landed at the tip of a peninsula

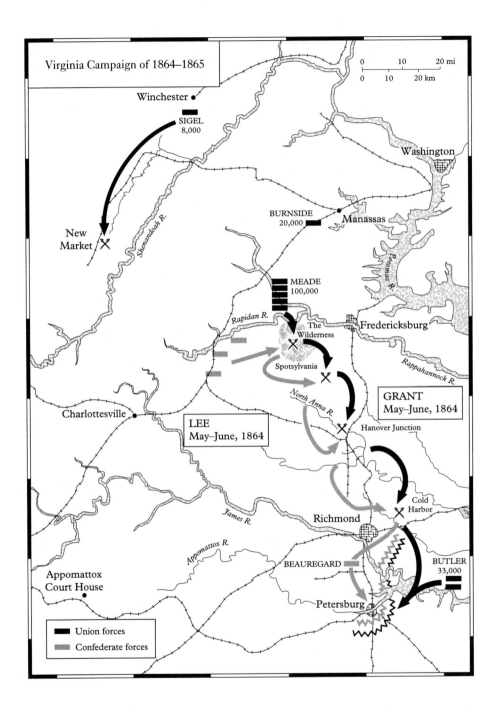

Virginia Campaign of 1864–1865

0   10   20 mi
0 10   20 km

Winchester

SIGEL
8,000

Washington

BURNSIDE
20,000   Manassas

New
Market

Shenandoah R.

MEADE
100,000

Rapidan R.

The
Wilderness

Fredericksburg

Rappahannock R.

Spotsylvania

GRANT
May–June, 1864

North Anna R.

Charlottesville

LEE
May–June, 1864

Hanover Junction

Cold
Harbor

James R.

Richmond

Appomattox R.

Appomattox
Court House

BEAUREGARD

BUTLER
33,000

Petersburg

Union forces
Confederate forces

formed by the James and Appomattox rivers, advanced a short distance inland, then stalled. A much smaller Confederate detachment soon sealed off the neck of the peninsula with entrenchments. This left Butler's force, in Grant's scornful words, "as completely shut off from further operations against Richmond as if it had been in a bottle strongly corked." Designed to place additional pressure on Lee and siphon troops from his army, these efforts to "hold a leg" wound up having the opposite effect: with Sigel beaten and Butler neutralized, Lee received 8,500 reinforcements from the forces that had opposed the two Union generals.

Lee's increased strength made "fighting it out" at Spotsylvania no longer such a good idea. Unable to dislodge the Confederate commander, Grant attempted once again to slide past Lee's right flank and continue his advance southward. The formula he had given Meade before the campaign—"Wherever Lee goes, there you will go also"—became reversed: wherever Grant went, Lee went also, and Lee invariably got there first. Yet in every previous campaign, Lee had found a way to wrest the initiative from his opponent. Grant gave him no such opportunity. The Union general-in-chief had both the military strength and the moral determination to keep moving on.

The campaign in progress resembled nothing that had come before. Previous Civil War operations had usually followed a fairly classic pattern: long periods of preliminary maneuver, careful sparring as the opposing forces located one another, then a major battle that ended in clear-cut victory or defeat. Grant's campaign, on the other hand, amounted to a six-week brawl in which the armies seldom broke contact for more than a few hours and from which no clear decision emerged. The losses it generated horrified the Northern population. In the long months since Shiloh the North had grown used to casualty lists on the same scale as those of that bloody struggle; but the fighting in May and early June 1864 produced 55,000 Union dead, wounded, and missing—about five times the cost of Shiloh. Confederate losses exceeded 20,000: much fewer than those of the Federals, but about the same in proportion to the forces engaged.

The campaign differed in one other respect as well. Both sides had learned the value of field fortifications; indeed, the soldiers had gotten so that they would dig in without orders and practically every time they halted for more than a few minutes. "It is a rule," wrote one Union officer, "that when the Rebels halt, the first day gives them a good rifle-pit; the second, a regular infantry parapet with artillery in position; and the third a parapet with abatis [sharpened stakes] in front and entrenched batteries behind. Sometimes they put this three days' work into the first twenty-four hours." These entrenchments had the effect of making it almost impossible to carry a defensive position; those who attempted it generally got slaughtered, while their killers found almost total protection behind rifle pits and earthen parapets.

Though the generals did not quickly grasp the full significance of this, the Battle of Cold Harbor provided a final, chilling lesson. By early June, Grant's army had gotten within seven miles of Richmond, but it had not yet beaten Lee's army and it had nearly run out of room to maneuver:

further efforts to turn the Confederates would run into the tidal estuary of the James River. Partly because of this situation, and partly because Grant thought he discerned a weakness in Lee's line, he ordered a frontal assault against Lee's entrenched defenses. The attack jumped off at about 4:30 A.M. on June 3. It was really nothing more than a succession of charges made along different parts of the line, most of which collapsed within minutes, smashed beneath an annihilating storm of rifle and artillery fire. The abortive and bloody attack cost nearly 7,000 Union casualties. Grant later called it one of two attacks during the war he wished he had not ordered.

With no prospect whatever of breaking through to Richmond, Grant then went forward with an operation he had pondered even while the armies were still fighting at Spotsylvania. He would shift the Army of the Potomac south of the James River, use the river as his line of supply, and try to get at Petersburg, a city about twenty miles south of Richmond through which the Confederate capital—and Lee's army—received most of its supplies. Between June 12 and 16 the Union forces made the crossing, with Grant managing the feat so adroitly that for several days Lee did not know what was being done. As a result the Army of the Potomac almost seized Petersburg before an adequate rebel force could arrive to hold the city. Through misperception and bad management on the part of Meade's subordinates, however, the fleeting opportunity vanished. Lee's army scrambled down to Petersburg, entered fortifications already in place to defend the city, and once again forced a stalemate. The Army of the Potomac settled in for a siege; for the next ten months, Lee and Grant faced one another across a trench-scarred landscape.

The Siege of Petersburg

Militarily the stalemate at Petersburg suited Grant just fine. Although ideally he would have preferred to destroy Lee's army outright, at a minimum he expected the Army of the Potomac's advance to pressure Lee so strongly that the Confederate would be unable to send any troops to support Johnston in his defense against Sherman. This the Army of the Potomac had accomplished. Sherman, meanwhile, was steadily pushing Johnston's army back toward Atlanta, and Grant regarded the Georgia offensive as crucial. Once Sherman had gained control of Atlanta, the entire Southern heartland would lay open, and therein lay the ultimate key to Union victory.

Politically, however, the stalemate in Virginia was sheer poison. Northerners considered it unacceptable that the bloody campaign to reach the Richmond-Petersburg area should have yielded nothing better than a deadlock. War weariness had set in, and although on the map the Union armies had made great gains, none of them seemed to have brought the conclusion of the struggle one whit nearer. Many Northerners began to feel that perhaps the only way to end the war lay in a negotiated, compromise peace. Worse, with the 1864 presidential election approaching, they might well register their discouragement at the polls if the stalemate continued.

Summer brought no reversal in Union fortunes. Grant could not get into Petersburg; Sherman drew nearer to Atlanta but found that the city's fortifications firmly barred entry. Meanwhile Lee managed what looked like a real victory: in June he detached a corps under Lieutenant General Jubal Early and sent him swinging northwest toward the Shenandoah Valley. After clearing the valley of Union troops, Early's men crossed into western Maryland, sliced southeast toward Washington, and by mid-July actually carried their raid to within sight of the Federal Capitol building. Although the Confederates could not penetrate the powerful fortifications that ringed Washington and Union reinforcements soon arrived to drive them away, this seemed less significant than the sheer fact that, in the summer of 1864, a major Confederate force could still successfully threaten the Union capital. Early's raid, coupled with the apparent lack of Union success in Virginia and Georgia, boded ill for the upcoming November election. In August 1864 Northern morale reached its nadir, and Lincoln gloomily predicted that he would shortly lose the presidency.

To Atlanta and Beyond

What saved Lincoln was the capture of Atlanta—another potent demonstration of the close connection between battlefield developments and politics. The chief author of his salvation was Major General William Tecumseh Sherman, Grant's most trusted lieutenant and his choice to head the Military Division of the Mississippi. The triumph came after four months of steady campaigning along the one-hundred-mile corridor that separated Chattanooga and Atlanta. It probably destroyed what remained of the Confederacy's chance to win the Civil War.

Northern Georgia

The Atlanta Campaign pitted Sherman against Joseph E. Johnston, the Confederate general chosen to replace Bragg after the humiliating Chattanooga fiasco. Sherman led approximately 100,000 men, divided into three parts: the Army of the Cumberland, commanded by Major General George H. Thomas; the Army of the Tennessee, led by Major General James B. McPherson; and the corps-sized Army of the Ohio, commanded by Major General John M. Schofield. To oppose the Union forces Johnston had just 50,000 men (although he was shortly reinforced to about 60,000). Although outnumbered, the Confederates had the advantage of fighting on the defensive in rugged mountain country well-suited to the purpose.

Ever since Chattanooga, the Confederate Army of Tennessee had been posted at Dalton, Georgia, and had strongly fortified Rocky Face Ridge just northwest of the town. Sherman called this position "the terrible door of death." A direct attack was out of the question. Instead, in early May he sent McPherson's army on a long swing around the rebel left flank while Thomas and Schofield distracted Johnston. McPherson managed to penetrate into the Confederate rear through a carelessly guarded mountain gap. This penetration forced Johnston to abandon his first line and retreat about ten miles to Resaca. Sherman had taken the first trick, but in retrospect he realized that McPherson had missed a great opportunity. Had he acted more aggressively he might have cut Johnston's line of retreat, but instead McPherson had obeyed the letter of Sherman's orders and avoided this daring but risky move. "Well, Mac," Sherman told his protegé, "you missed the opportunity of your life."

The rival armies lingered three days at Resaca while Sherman vainly searched for a weakness in Johnston's line. Finding none, he sent McPherson on a second wide sweep around the Confederate left flank. This time Johnston withdrew another twenty-five miles until he reached Cassville on May 19. Thus, in twelve days' time the Army of Tennessee had yielded about half the distance from Dalton to Atlanta. President Jefferson Davis was considerably disgruntled by this development, but given the great disparity in troop strength Johnston felt he had little choice.

One of his key subordinates disagreed, however. Lieutenant General John B. Hood, a former division commander in the Army of Northern Virginia, had come west during Longstreet's September 1863 redeployment and had remained with the Army of Tennessee. A gallant fighter—he had lost an arm at Gettysburg and a leg at Chickamauga—Hood had been befriended by President Davis and his wife and had been given command of a corps in the Army of Tennessee. He knew Davis and Johnston despised one another and, as a good Davis ally, sent the president a stream of private letters critical of the army commander. Trained in the offensive school of warfare favored by Lee, Hood considered Johnston far too cautious. Sherman, he believed, should be dealt a whole-souled counterpunch of the sort that had bested McClellan, Pope, and Hooker. Davis agreed and considered relieving Johnston of command if he continued to retreat.

Johnston, however, remained true to his Fabian tactics. (Ironically, on the one occasion when he did plan a counterstroke, Hood proved unready and urged that the attack be called off.) The Army of Tennessee occupied one well-entrenched defensive position after another. Sherman, meanwhile, made yet another swing around the Confederate left flank. The move brought him a few miles closer to Atlanta but no closer to "breaking up" Johnston's army as Grant had instructed.

Unfortunately for Sherman, his three armies relied for supply on a single railroad coming down from Chattanooga. Johnston destroyed the railroad as he withdrew and although Sherman's engineers quickly repaired the damage, Sherman realized the vulnerability of this line. He particularly feared that Confederate cavalry raiders—especially the fearsome Bedford Forrest—might damage his communications in Tennessee, and he diverted thousands of Union troops to forestall them. Consequently, instead of making Confederate raids, Forrest spent the summer of 1864 largely responding to Federal raids into Mississippi. The tactic worked: although Forrest racked

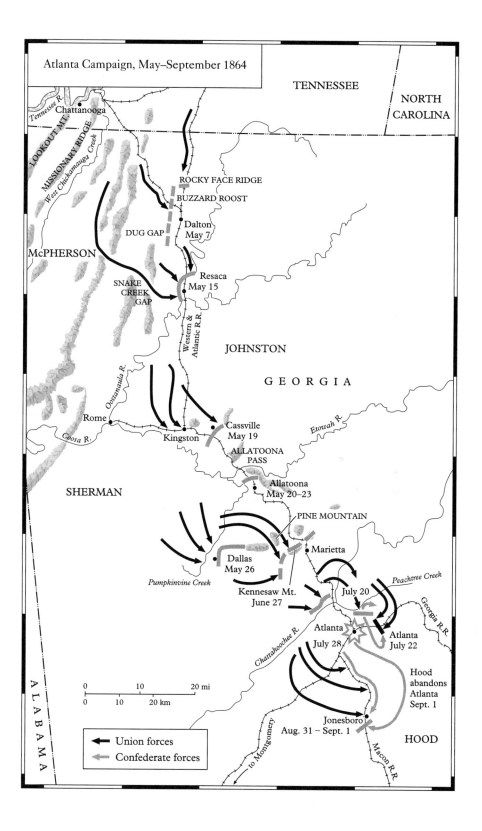

Atlanta Campaign, May–September 1864

TENNESSEE

NORTH CAROLINA

Tennessee R.
Chattanooga

LOOKOUT MT.
MISSIONARY RIDGE
West Chickamauga Creek

ROCKY FACE RIDGE

BUZZARD ROOST

McPHERSON

DUG GAP
Dalton
May 7

Resaca
May 15

SNAKE CREEK GAP

Western & Atlantic R.R.

JOHNSTON

GEORGIA

Oostanaula R.

Rome

Coosa R.

Kingston

Cassville
May 19

Etowah R.

ALLATOONA PASS

SHERMAN

Allatoona
May 20–23

PINE MOUNTAIN

Marietta

Dallas
May 26

Pumpkinvine Creek

Kennesaw Mt.
June 27

July 20

Peachtree Creek

Georgia R.R.

Chattahoochee R.

Atlanta
July 28

Atlanta
July 22

Hood abandons Atlanta Sept. 1

A L A B A M A

0   10   20 mi
0   10   20 km

to Montgomery

Jonesboro
Aug. 31 – Sept. 1

Macon R.R.

HOOD

⬅ Union forces
➡ Confederate forces

up an impressive series of victories against these raiding forces, he was forced to leave Sherman's communications alone.

For the first two months of the Atlanta Campaign neither side risked a major battle. As a result, neither side lost heavily; the Union armies, indeed, suffered casualties only marginally greater than the Confederates. Finally, on June 27, Sherman mounted a major assault upon Johnston's center at Kennesaw Mountain. This part of the Confederate line appeared weak to Sherman, who thought a breakthrough might be possible. Moreover, recent rains had reduced his army's mobility so that the alternative to an attack was delay. Then too, Sherman believed, "The enemy as well as my own army had settled down to the belief that flanking alone was my game." By attacking, he hoped to convince Johnston that he might strike anywhere and thus that Johnston must hold his entire line in strength. He also thought it would restore some aggressiveness to his own troops. They had become so chary of fortifications, he complained, that a "fresh furrow in a plowed field will stop a whole column, and all begin to entrench." But the Battle of Kennesaw Mountain cost his army 2,000 casualties, against just 450 for the Confederates, and gained not an inch of ground.

Sherman then reverted to the flanking game. He made a fourth move around Johnston's left flank, breached the line of the Chattahoochee River—the last real barrier separating him from Atlanta—and followed up with a fifth turning movement, this time around the Confederate right flank. By mid-July, Johnston had withdrawn behind the outer fortifications that ringed the city itself. Although the Army of Tennessee remained intact, it had run out of room to maneuver.

Battles for Atlanta

At about this time a visiting congressional delegation warned Johnston that Davis would surely remove him if he continued his passive defense. Artlessly, one of the congressmen quoted a story that was then making the rounds in Richmond, to the effect that the president had said that "if he were in your place he could whip Sherman now." "Yes," Johnston harrumphed. "I know Mr. Davis thinks he can do a great many things other men would hesitate to attempt. For instance, he tried to do what God failed to do. He tried to make a soldier of Braxton Bragg, and you know the result. It couldn't be done."

Johnston might have heeded the delegation's warning. On July 17, Davis removed him and substituted Hood. He made the change despite misgivings expressed by Lee, who of course had once commanded Hood. Asked for his opinion, Lee was candid: "It is a bad time to release the commander of an army situated as that of Tennessee. We may lose Atlanta and the army too. Hood is a bold fighter. I am doubtful as to other qualities necessary." In perhaps the most controversial military decision Davis made during the war, he went ahead with the replacement anyway. Johnston, despite his excessive caution, had been a canny tactician and frugal with his limited supply of manpower. Hood did exactly what the president wanted:

As this photo attests, the Confederate manufacturing center of Atlanta, Georgia, was one of the most heavily fortified cities in America by mid-1864. Its capture by Sherman's army in September 1864 electrified the North, dismayed the South, and helped ensure Lincoln's reelection two months later.

he fought. The result, as Lee had suspected, was the loss of Atlanta and the crippling of Hood's army.

On July 19, Hood struck the Union Army of the Cumberland while its two sister armies were attempting another of their inevitable turning movements. He achieved little. Two days later he struck again, this time against McPherson's Army of the Tennessee. The attack was adroitly made, but as usual the defending side had the resilience and flexibility to recover and restore the line. A third assault on July 28 resulted in a virtual massacre. Although McPherson was killed in one of these battles (one of only two army commanders to suffer such a fate), Hood's army lost about 15,000 of its 40,000 effectives; Federal casualties numbered just 5,400.

Hood, like his predecessor, now withdrew into the Atlanta fortifications. Sherman inaugurated a quasi-siege, lobbing shells into the beleaguered city, and meanwhile planned to cut the railroads connecting Atlanta with the rest of the South. In late August he carried out this operation. Leaving one corps to distract Hood, he took the rest of his armies on one last turning movement, this time to a point well south of the city. Hood recognized the move and turned to meet it, but he was too late. Sherman had gotten squarely across the Confederate line of communications. When a desperate Confederate counterstroke at Jonesboro failed to dislodge Sherman, Hood had no choice but to abandon the city. It fell on September 2, 1864.

Hood's army, badly weakened, drew off into northern Alabama and tried with limited success to destroy Sherman's extended supply lines.

The fall of Atlanta sealed the fate of the Confederacy. Until then the possibility existed that Lincoln would lose his bid for reelection that year because the North, like the South, had grown increasingly frustrated with a war that seemed to go on interminably. If Lincoln lost, it seemed likely that some sort of negotiated peace might be arranged. But Sherman's victory gave Union morale an enormous boost. The North now was clearly winning.

Union Raids

September brought additional triumphs. In the middle of that month, a Union army under Major General Philip H. Sheridan confronted Early's veterans in the Shenandoah Valley. Badly outnumbered, the Confederates suffered defeat in two sharp battles that forced them to yield the entire valley to Union domination. In October, Sheridan won a third shattering victory that destroyed Early's army for good, but by that time the valley that Early defended had already become "a smoking, barren waste." Its destruction illustrates an important dimension of Grant's strategy.

General Philip H. Sheridan was one of the Union's most implacable "hard war" generals. As commander of Northern forces in the Shenandoah Valley, he defeated the Confederates in two sharp battles, then destroyed the valley's barns and crops to end its days as a source of Confederate supply.

Sometimes called the "breadbasket of the Confederacy," the rich Shenandoah Valley had long served as a major source of supply to Lee's army. Consequently, Grant regarded destruction of the Valley as a legitimate military objective. Once Early's force had been beaten, he believed, the pursuing troops should "eat out Virginia clear and clean as far as they go, so that crows flying over it for the balance of the season will have to carry their provender with them." As he explained to Sheridan, "[N]othing should be left to invite the enemy to return. Take all provisions, forage and stock wanted for the use of your command. Such as cannot be consumed, destroy."

During the early weeks of autumn Sheridan carried out these instructions with grim enthusiasm. By mid-October he could report, "I have destroyed over 2,000 barns filled with wheat, hay and farming implements; over 70 mills, filled with flour and wheat; have driven in front of the army over 4,000 head of stock, and have killed and issued to the troops not less than 3,000 sheep. . . . The people here are getting sick of the war."

The final sentence in Sheridan's dispatch alluded to a new element in the struggle, one that Grant had begun to see as early as 1862 but that had required two more years to reach maturity. The war for the Union had become not only a war against the "slave aristocracy" but against the Southern people as a whole. Typical of this tough new mindset was Sherman's decision, shortly after his capture of Atlanta, to order the evacuation of its entire civilian population. When the city's mayor protested the inhumanity of this action, Sherman responded witheringly: "[M]y orders are not designed to meet the humanities of the case but to prepare for the future struggles. . . . War is cruelty, and you cannot refine it. . . . You might as well appeal against the thunder storm as against these terrible hardships of war." Although Grant never came close to Sherman's desolating eloquence, his own orders as well as his endorsement of Sherman demonstrate that he felt exactly the same way.

For several weeks after the fall of Atlanta, Sherman made no further advances. He was too busy protecting his greatly overextended supply line. No longer obliged to defend Atlanta, Hood had shifted into northwest Georgia and now drew his supplies from neighboring Alabama. With his own lines of communication secure, Hood spent October threatening the vulnerable Western and Atlantic Railroad that was Sherman's lifeline with the North. Sherman's armies spent several frustrating weeks fruitlessly chasing Hood's army as it bedeviled the tenuous Union supply line through the northern part of the state. The Federals, in effect, were having to fight twice for the same real estate.

Clearly some new solution must be found, and Sherman believed he knew what it was. He wanted to cut loose from the Western and Atlantic Railroad entirely, abandon Atlanta, and strike out for a new base on the coast. On October 9 he wrote Grant, "I propose that we break up the railroad from Chattanooga forward, and that we strike out with our wagons for Milledgeville, Macon, and Savannah." The mere occupation of Georgia, he argued, was useless given the hostile population. "[B]ut the utter destruction of its [rail]roads, houses, and people, will cripple their military resources. . . . I can make the march, and make Georgia howl!"

Grant delayed before giving Sherman permission for the operation. Noting that the Confederate leadership might send Hood's army to recover middle Tennessee, he thought it best to eliminate Hood before doing anything else. Lincoln, for his part, confessed that Sherman's idea made him "anxious, if not actually fearful." But Sherman stuck to his guns. He could detach enough troops to protect Tennessee, he argued, and in any event the change of base could accomplish an important purpose in its own right. "If we can march a well-appointed army right through his territory," Sherman argued, "it is a demonstration to the world, foreign and domestic, that we have a power which [Confederate President Jefferson] Davis cannot resist. This may not be war but rather statesmanship; nevertheless it is overwhelming to my mind that there are thousands of people abroad and in the South who reason thus: if the North can march an army right through the South, it is proof positive that the North can prevail. . . ."

Eventually Grant approved Sherman's proposal. Sherman sent about 35,000 troops under General George Thomas to defend Tennessee, then abandoned Atlanta after destroying everything that might support the Confederate war effort. On November 15, advancing against almost no opposition, Sherman and 60,000 veterans began to carve a sixty-mile swath across Georgia. "[W]e had a gay old campaign," declared one of his men. "Destroyed all we could not eat, stole their niggers [sic], burned their cotton & gins, spilled their sorghum, burned & twisted their R. Roads and raised Hell generally."

By Christmas Eve 1864, Sherman had entered the city of Savannah on the Atlantic coast. In February 1865 he headed northward into the Carolinas, repeating on an even grander scale the pattern of his March to the Sea. Ultimately these marches, more than anything else, destroyed the Confederacy. They ruined Southern morale, smashed the remainder of the Confederate rail network, eliminated foodstuffs and war resources, and caused the desertion of thousands of Confederate soldiers who had resisted valiantly for years.

The Naval War, 1862–1865

Shortly after Sherman's army began its march northward into the Carolinas, a Union fleet appeared off Fort Fisher, North Carolina. This sprawling, improvised earthwork commanded the approaches to Wilmington, the last Confederate port open to blockade runners. When, on February 22, 1865, a combined landing party of 6,000 Federal soldiers and sailors successfully stormed the fort, it marked the culmination of a four-year naval campaign aimed at isolating the South from the outside world.

Until 1861, the U.S. Navy had played only a peripheral role in America's wars. During both the War for American Independence and the War of

1812, the Royal Navy had easily predominated; American naval contributions were confined to commerce raiding, a few single-ship encounters, and showing the flag in neutral ports. During the Civil War, however, the U.S. Navy for the first time bore a major strategic responsibility. Not only was it expected to control the open sea—a relatively simple task—it was also required to maintain a close blockade of the Confederate shore, to transport Union military might wherever it was needed, and to fight for control of the Confederate inland waters.

Since the American navy had never before faced such a task, it obviously had to improvise. But at least it had the advantage of existing when the war began. The Confederate navy also had to improvise, but more than that, it also had to create itself and devise a coherent mission under the immediate pressures of war. Although both sides did well with the resources available, the disparity in industrial might between North and South was never more lopsided than in the contest between the two navies. The North had an enormous advantage throughout the conflict. The South was never able to mount a serious challenge to Union seapower.

The Blockade

Sheer numbers convey something of the North's advantage. In April 1861 the Federal government possessed about ninety warships. By December 1864, under the outstanding leadership of Secretary of the Navy Gideon Welles, the North had expanded this total to 671 vessels, including 236 steam-powered ships constructed during the war. Although much of this new navy was used in riverine warfare and to track down commerce raiders, most of it went to enforce the Union blockade.

The blockade served two important functions. First, in economic terms it greatly reduced the South's access to outside markets, making the import and export of goods much more difficult. Second, diplomatically it helped reinforce a sense of the North's iron determination to crush the rebellion and caused European powers to think long and hard before recognizing the Confederacy. But maintaining the blockade was certainly a huge task. The rebellious states had a combined shoreline of roughly 3,000 miles, with 189 inlets and river mouths into which a blockade runner might dart. Blockade duty was dreary. Months might pass without action; during that time the main enemies were discomfort and boredom. One naval officer tried to give his mother some idea of the rigors of blockading duty: "[G]o to the roof on a hot summer day," he advised, "talk to a half-dozen degenerates, descend to the basement, drink tepid water full of iron rust, climb to the roof again, and repeat the process at intervals until [you are] fagged out, then go to bed with everything shut tight."

When a blockade runner was sighted, it enjoyed every advantage. Typically such a vessel would choose a moonless night to make its run, during which time its slate-gray hull would be nearly invisible. Swift and almost silent, the blockade runners would also burn smoke-free anthracite coal to heighten the difficulty of sighting them and would sometimes fire decoy signal flares to mislead the blockaders. Such tactics, coupled with an intimate knowledge of the shoal waters just outside the harbor entrances, resulted in a high rate of success. By one estimate, 84 percent of the runners that attempted the port of Wilmington made it through (1,735 out of 2,054), with a similar ratio prevailing along the rest of the Confederate coastline.

Some historians offer these figures as evidence of the blockade's ineffectiveness. Others, however, maintain that such statistics miss the point. The true measure of comparison, they maintain, should be difference in Southern sea trade before the war and during it. By this criterion the blockade was quite effective. Twenty thousand vessels cleared in or out of Southern ports in the years 1857–1860, compared with just 8,000 during the entire Civil War. Moreover, since blockade runners typically carried less cargo than an average merchantman, the wartime tonnage of goods imported or exported was probably less than one-third of the prewar figure.

That still leaves the question of the role played by the blockade in inflicting Confederate defeat. Here statistics have much less meaning. The issue turns, in part, on such intangibles as the blockade's impact on the Confederacy's morale. A more concrete way to look at the matter is to note the concern (or lack thereof) with which the Confederate government regarded the blockade. Certainly it never saw breaking the blockade as a priority (even if this were in its power, which it was not), and as late as 1864 the government required that only one-half the blockade runners' space be given over to military cargo. Then too, it is difficult to see what the Confederacy required that it could not produce. Food? It had plenty of that; the difficulty there lay in shipping local surpluses to points of need via the Confederacy's inadequate rolling stock. Arms and ammunition? The Confederacy, under the able leadership of ordnance czar Josiah Gorgas, managed to supply these wants to the end of the war.

Ultimately one must concede that the blockade was scarcely decisive in its own right. Still it did have an effect—not just in terms of reducing the South's volume of trade but also in terms of exacerbating high prices for consumer goods that helped fuel a ruinous inflation. But the Confederacy had enough territory to provide for its own needs—and did an ingenious job of exploiting its resources. Perhaps, then, the Union navy's most pronounced contribution to victory came in the support it gave the land forces.

Joint Operations and Riverine Warfare

Throughout the war the Union exploited its great superiority in sea power to throw troops ashore at various points along the Confederate coastline. These operations scarcely resembled the amphibious warfare of World War II, for in the great majority of cases they met little or no opposition directly on the beaches. It was much more usual for the troops to go ashore unopposed, establish a solid, fortified enclave, and only then advance inland. On only two important occasions during the conflict did troops try to fight their way ashore. The first, a Union night attack on Fort Sumter in September 1863, failed miserably. The second, against Fort Fisher in January 1865, was of course a success.

The relative dearth of opposed landings owed mainly to the fact that much of the Confederate coastline was undefended. The rebels maintained troops and artillery only at a few dozen key points. Thus it was easy for Union forces to find places to land without having to fight simply to get ashore. Their troubles came later, for although Union troops had little difficulty establishing a coastal enclave, they found it far more difficult to penetrate very far inland. For one thing, once the Union troops were ashore the Confederates knew exactly where they were and could dispatch sufficient troops to block them. The more important reason, however, was that there were almost never enough Union troops based along the coast to undertake offensive action.

Indeed, for most of the conflict the Lincoln administration neglected to use ocean-based sea power as a major instrument in the land war. McClellan's Peninsula Campaign appears to have permanently soured Lincoln, Stanton, and Halleck on this option. When Grant proposed in January 1864 that 60,000 troops be dispatched to occupied North Carolina, whence to raid the railroads that supplied Richmond, the administration vetoed the plan.

If one excepts the Peninsula Campaign—which functioned, in most respects, like a conventional land campaign—the most sustained joint operation of the war was the siege of Charleston, South Carolina. Although this campaign nominally began as early as November 1861, it did not start in earnest until April 1863, when a Union flotilla composed entirely of ironclads tried to bombard the Charleston forts into submission. The forts pummeled them instead, achieving over 400 direct hits—without, however, doing great injury to the heavily armored vessels. Then throughout the balance of 1863, the army and navy cooperated in a series of attacks upon the forts, but achieved limited success. The geography of Charleston harbor made it an extraordinarily difficult nut to crack. Both the entrance and the approach channel were narrow, so that Union warships had little room to maneuver, while forts protecting the harbor were themselves protected by salt marshes and swamps. Indeed the prolonged campaign was almost certainly a venture not worth the gain, except that Charleston had been the original cockpit of secession and many Northerners ached to see it destroyed. (The city fell only in February 1865, after Sherman's advancing army had cut its communications with the rest of the South.)

In contrast to the relatively limited cooperation between land forces and the bluewater navy, the army and brownwater navy worked hand-in-glove throughout the war. The two services cooperated effectively to reduce Forts Henry and Donelson, Island No. 10, Vicksburg, and a number of lesser Confederate fortresses in the Mississippi valley. Union naval control of the navigable rivers enabled land forces to supply themselves far from their main bases, and the riverine lines of communication proved much more difficult for rebels to disrupt than the highly vulnerable railroads. Moreover Federal gunboats could also interdict long stretches of these rivers, rendering it next to impossible for large Confederate forces to cross. This interdiction significantly impeded Southern mobility, particularly in terms of transferring units across the Mississippi River.

The most striking feature of the coastal and riverine war was the use made of ironclad vessels. When the war broke out the American navy possessed no armored ships of any kind; only Britain and France owned a few experimental ironclads. The Confederacy, however, soon began to construct an ironclad using the hull of the captured frigate USS *Merrimack*, partially scuttled when the Federals abandoned the Norfolk Navy Yard in April 1861. Rechristened the CSS *Virginia*, the new ironclad rode so low in the water that it resembled the roof of a floating barn. It mounted ten 11-inch cannon and, in a throwback to the days of galleys, an iron ram on the bow below the waterline.

Designed to break the Union blockade and protect the James River estuary, the *Virginia* briefly struck terror in Union hearts. During its maiden voyage on March 8, 1862, it steamed from Norfolk into Hampton Roads, rammed one Union frigate, destroyed another with gunfire, and ran a third warship aground before retiring for the night. The next day it steamed forth to wreak further havoc, only to be confronted by an oddly shaped vessel that looked exactly like a cheesebox on a raft. It was in fact the USS *Monitor*, the North's answer to the *Virginia* and a remarkable answer at that. Created by the brilliant naval designer John Ericsson, the heavily armored *Monitor* boasted no fewer than forty patentable inventions, most prominently a rotating turret (the "cheesebox") that mounted two 11-inch smoothbore cannon

In March 1862, the USS *Monitor* clashed with the CSS *Virginia* at Hampton Roads, Virginia, in the world's first battle between ironclad warships. Although the combat ended in a draw, the *Monitor* caused the *Virginia* to return to port, thereby saving Union wooden warships in the area from further damage.

and could fire in any direction. Built in just one hundred days, the Union ironclad managed to wallow down from New York City just in time to save the fleet in Hampton Roads from complete disaster. In a two-hour battle on March 9, the two revolutionary vessels pumped shot after shot at one another, only to see the heavy cannon balls merely dent the enemy's armor and ricochet into the sea. Neither ship was seriously hurt, although the *Virginia* eventually broke off the action and withdrew into Norfolk harbor. Two months later it was scuttled to prevent capture when the Confederates withdrew from the area. (The *Monitor* eventually sank in heavy seas in December 1862.)

Both the *Virginia* and the *Monitor* served as prototypes for further armored vessels. The South ultimately built twenty-one ironclads (and laid the keels for twenty-nine more), mostly patterned after the *Virginia*. The North, which constructed fifty-eight ironclads, tried several designs but concentrated on vessels patterned after the *Monitor*. Every one of these ships was intended either for coastal defense or attack; none fought in the open ocean. Together they confirmed a major technological shift in naval warfare. As the London *Times* remarked shortly after the fight at Hampton Roads, the British navy had suddenly dropped from having 149 first-class warships to exactly two, its twin experimental ironclads. Apart from those two, "[t]here is not now a ship in the English navy . . . that it would not be madness to trust in an engagement with that little *Monitor*."

Commerce Raiders

In addition to its ironclads, the South also built, or purchased, a number of commerce raiders, the perennial resort of weaker maritime powers. It tried privateers as well—privately owned vessels given "letters of marque" and permitted to attack enemy shipping. In older times privateering was a lucrative business, but most European powers had officially disowned the practice by the mid-nineteenth century, and would-be privateers found it too difficult to bring captured prizes into Southern ports. Thus the Confederacy had to use warships manned by regular naval crews and designed primarily to destroy, not capture, enemy merchantmen.

The South deployed only a relative handful of commerce raiders, but they achieved great notoriety and in some respects great effectiveness. They sank a large number of Union merchantmen, forced hundreds more to seek refuge by reregistering under neutral flags, and sent insurance premiums soaring. The CSS *Shenandoah* managed to cripple the New England whaling fleet in the Bering Sea—it did this, incidentally, in June 1865, unaware that the war was over—but the greatest rebel sea raider was the CSS *Alabama*, commanded by the rakish Captain Raphael Semmes.

Like many Confederate commerce raiders, the *Alabama* was built in England, having been covertly commissioned by the tireless Confederate agent, James Bulloch. (Bulloch also tried to get British shipyards to build several ironclads as well, but Her Majesty's government eventually blocked the attempt.) The warship mounted eight guns and could make better than

Although the Confederacy could not begin to match the Union's naval might, it still managed to deploy a number of commerce raiders, including the CSS *Nashville*, shown here burning a captured Northern merchant vessel.

thirteen knots under steam. In its twenty-two-month voyage it destroyed a total of sixty-eight Union vessels—without, however, injuring the crews. Instead the rebel sailors (many of them actually British subjects) boarded the enemy merchantmen, removed whatever they wanted, and took their seamen prisoner. Only then would the enemy vessels be burned or blown up. When the *Alabama* grew too overcrowded with reluctant guests, Semmes would designate the next captured merchantman a "cartel ship," place the prisoners aboard, and let them sail to the nearest port. In that way he accomplished his mission without bloodshed.

The *Alabama* continued its colorful career until June 1864, when the Union frigate USS *Kearsage* cornered the raider while it was in a French harbor for repairs. The *Kearsage* hovered outside the entrance to the port, barring escape. The *Alabama* gamely came forth to do battle, but in a spirited one-hour engagement the Confederate vessel was sunk. Semmes himself went over the side, was picked up by a yacht filled with admiring sightseers, and thus eluded capture.

The commerce raiders exerted a surprising influence on subsequent naval policy. After the war the American navy regarded them as a vindication of its historic emphasis on raiding as opposed to major fleet actions. Despite his own wartime experience with ironclads, Admiral David Dixon Porter led the U.S. Navy throughout the 1870s in its continuing rejection of a battle-fleet orientation. "[O]ne vessel like the *Alabama* roaming the ocean, sinking and destroying," he wrote, "would do more to bring about peace than a dozen unwieldy iron-clads. . . ." Some European navies concurred. Inspired in part by the exploits of Confederate raiders, many French and Italian navalists touted a maritime strategy that emphasized coastal defense and commerce destruction. In any event, not until the 1890s would the United States move decisively toward a naval strategy based unequivocally on the battleship and command of the sea.

All in all, the naval conflict remained a constant and indispensable feature of the Civil War. But the two contending forces compiled very different records. Stephen R. Mallory, the South's highly capable secretary of the navy, certainly did a superb job of creating a navy, yet it must be questioned whether this navy managed to achieve results commensurate even with the relatively slender resources expended on it. The ironclad program produced a number of formidable vessels but usually failed to prevent Union warships from capturing a Southern port when they mounted a major effort to do so. Land fortifications, not armored vessels, seemed the most effective way to defend Southern harbors. The commerce raiders, for their part, did considerable damage but never enough even to deflate the North's will to continue the war. Considering the vast amount of commerce carried by Northern ships, Southern raiders were really little more than a nuisance.

By contrast, the Union navy played a major role in defeating the Confederacy. Union blockaders sharply curtailed the amount of Confederate shipping and may have contributed to a decline in Southern morale. Union gunboats and ironclads vied with their rebel counterparts for control of Southern rivers, sounds, and ports. The Union naval contribution richly deserved Lincoln's wry compliment to Federal seamen in 1863: "At all the watery margins they have been present. Not only on the deep blue sea, the broad bay, the rapid river, but also up the narrow muddy bayou, and wherever the ground was a little damp, they have made their tracks."

The War Ends

Sherman's marches were only the largest of many Union raids that characterized the final six months of the conflict. The Federals, in essence, had abandoned any attempt to hold Southern territory. Instead they simply ravaged it, destroying anything of military use and in the process convincing thousands of white Southerners that the Confederate government could not protect them. The Davis administration, meanwhile, grew increasingly out of touch with the darkening strategic picture. Instead, in the autumn of 1864, Davis made an energetic circuit of the Deep South and argued that if the Southern people would only redouble their efforts, the Confederacy might yet plant its banners on the banks of the Ohio. This visionary thinking actually produced one of the strangest campaigns of the war, Hood's disastrous invasion of Tennessee.

Franklin and Nashville

Conceived in early October 1864, Hood's operation had two main purposes. Strategically it was supposed to recover middle Tennessee and cut off Sherman from the North; Hood even fantasized that he might eventually combine with Lee's army and overwhelm Grant. Politically it was intended to bolster flagging Southern morale; Jefferson Davis hinted on several occasions that Hood's thrust might reach as far as the Ohio River. The fulfillment of either objective was clearly well beyond the reach of Confederate resources.

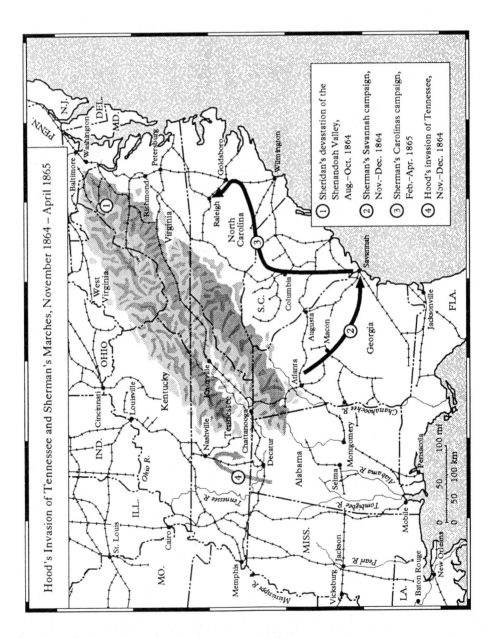

Hood's Invasion of Tennessee and Sherman's Marches, November 1864 – April 1865

① Sheridan's devastation of the Shenandoah Valley, Aug.–Oct. 1864

② Sherman's Savannah campaign, Nov.–Dec. 1864

③ Sherman's Carolinas campaign, Feb.–Apr. 1865

④ Hood's invasion of Tennessee, Nov.–Dec. 1864

For one thing, Hood lacked anywhere near enough troops to do the job. For another, he was not able to begin his campaign until mid-November, by which time his well-advertised invasion had brought thousands of Union troops into position to oppose him.

Even so, the Tennessee gambit gave the Union high command a fairly acute case of heartburn. Grant fretted that Hood's eccentric expedition might somehow disrupt his otherwise promising plans to finish off the Confederacy. Thomas, the Federal commander tapped to oppose Hood, believed the quality of Hood's veterans much superior to that of his own men, many of whom were either recently enlisted or garrison troops with little combat experience. (Thousands of his own veterans had either left the service by this time or had been retained by Sherman for his march to the sea.) Grant wanted Hood stopped as quickly as possible, before he had time to do mischief. Thomas, on the other hand, considered it best simply to delay Hood while he gathered his disparate forces into some kind of cohesive whole.

As a result, Thomas concentrated most of his troops at Nashville. In the meantime he sent Major General John M. Schofield, with 28,000 troops, to delay the Confederate advance. Hood managed to make an end run around Schofield's flank and came close to gobbling up the entire Union force. But somehow his army failed to strike Schofield, and the Federals retreated intact to Franklin, about thirty miles south of Nashville. There Hood caught up with them. Although the obvious move was to turn Schofield's flank again, Hood—enraged by his army's failure—ordered a frontal assault on November 30. In a larger and even more disastrous attack than Pickett's Charge at Gettysburg, 18,000 Confederates lunged into the teeth of Union field entrenchments, artillery, and rapid-fire carbines. More than half of them became casualties. Five Confederate generals lay among the dead.

The Battle of Franklin shattered whatever offensive potential Hood's army retained. Now reduced to about 30,000 men, its remnants continued to the outskirts of Nashville, which after thirty-one months of Union occupation was one of the most heavily fortified places on earth. Behind the scowling entrenchments were about 70,000 Federal troops. Though Hood made a feeble show at "besieging" the city, he had no chance for success.

Despite his formidable numerical advantage, Thomas delayed two full weeks before delivering the counterstroke, largely because of a major ice storm. But on December 15 the weather broke and Thomas attacked. After effectively deceiving Hood about the location of his main thrust, Thomas executed a massive flank attack that by nightfall overwhelmed the Confederate left. The following morning he put Hood's entire army to flight. On both days, massed Federal cavalry played a pivotal role in providing the speed and power necessary to achieve success and pursued Hood tirelessly for several days afterward. Although the casualties were not especially high—the Union forces lost about 3,000 men, the Confederates about 7,000 (three-fourths of them captured)—the Army of Tennessee practically went out of existence, leaving Lee's army as the Confederacy's only substantial remaining military force.

In March 1865, Lincoln met with Sherman, Grant, and Admiral David D. Porter aboard the USS *River Queen* to discuss the closing operations against the Confederacy. Here the president listens as Sherman recounts his destructive marches through Georgia and the Carolinas.

The Collapse of the Confederacy

In the waning months of the war, large columns of swiftly moving Union horsemen slashed through the Confederacy almost at will, crippling what remained of its railroad grid, burning war factories, and spreading despair among the Southern population. Meanwhile the Army of the Potomac patiently maintained its siege of Petersburg. As the long months passed, Grant extended his lines steadily to the west, never quite able to get around Lee's flank but forcing the Confederates to stretch their lines to the breaking point. In March 1865, Sheridan came from the Shenandoah Valley with most of his cavalry. Grant gave him an infantry corps and told him to break Lee's western flank. On April 1, in the Battle of Five Forks, Sheridan did exactly that. As soon as he learned of the victory, Grant ordered a general attack all along the Petersburg front. This final assault forced Lee to abandon the city, which fell on April 3. Union troops entered Richmond the same day.

Lee had only one move remaining: he could try to get his army—now reduced to barely 50,000 men—into central North Carolina, where Joseph E. Johnston with 20,000 troops was fruitlessly attempting to halt Sherman's advance north from Savannah. Grant understood this perfectly, and as he placed the Army of the Potomac in pursuit he made certain that Sheridan's cavalry thwarted every attempt by Lee to turn southward. As a result, Lee was forced to retreat to the west, hoping to reach a Confederate supply dump at Lynchburg, reprovision his famished men, and then somehow get into North Carolina.

On April 6 Union forces caught up with Lee's rear guard and destroyed it, capturing 6,000 prisoners. The following day Grant sent Lee a summons to surrender. Lee declined, but by the evening of April 8, Sheridan managed to get ahead of the beleaguered Confederate army and cut off its retreat. After one last effort to open an escape route—valiantly made but easily repulsed—Lee felt he had no choice but to surrender. On April 9, 1865, Palm Sunday, he requested a conference with Grant. The two commanders met at Appomattox Court House, a small village about eighty miles west of Richmond. There, in the parlor of a modest two-story home, Lee surrendered the Army of Northern Virginia. Early that evening, as word of the surrender spread like wildfire and Union soldiers began to cheer and touch off cannon in salutes to the victory, Grant told his staff officers to put a stop to the celebrations at once. "The war is over," he told them. "The Rebels are our countrymen again."

Although magnanimous, Grant's declaration was also premature. Some rebels continued to resist, among them Jefferson Davis. Not yet ready to submit, Davis had told the Southern people on April 4 that the war had merely entered a "new phase": "Relieved from the necessity of guarding cities and particular points, . . . with our army free to move from point to point, and strike in detail the detachments and garrisons of the enemy, . . . nothing is now needed to render our triumph certain, but the exhibition of our own unquenchable resolve. Let us but will it, and we are free."

Davis and his cabinet fled Richmond and established a new temporary capital at Danville, Virginia. Then, on the afternoon of April 10, he learned that Lee had surrendered at Appomattox Court House the previous day. The news, wrote Secretary of the Navy Stephen Mallory, "fell upon the ears of all like a firebell in the night." Later that evening, Davis and his cabinet left by train for Greensboro, North Carolina. Their famous "flight into oblivion" had begun.

Still determined, Davis met with Beauregard and Johnston and told them that the army could be fleshed out by gathering conscripts and deserters. Both men found this suggestion utterly devoid of realism; in a second meeting the next day, Johnston bluntly informed Davis that "it would be the greatest of human crimes for us to attempt to continue the war." After a prolonged silence, Davis asked for Beauregard's opinion. Beauregard basically agreed with Johnston; so, it turned out, did most of those present.

Afterward the discussion turned to the question of possible surrender terms. Davis still seemed not to grasp the enormity of the occasion, for the terms he suggested substantially failed to acknowledge that the South had lost the war. Realizing that the Federals would not treat with him, however, he authorized Johnston to carry out the negotiations. Yet even so, he obviously thought the contest could be continued and asked Johnston to give his favored line of retreat so that supplies could be stockpiled along the route. The hopelessness of the situation became apparent, however, when a dispatch from Lee arrived, officially announcing his surrender. Until that moment, Davis had seemed at ease and confident. But after reading it, he passed it along and "silently wept bitter tears."

While Johnston opened negotiations with Sherman, Davis and his cabinet made preparations to continue their flight. The president had a vague idea of making it to Alabama, where Confederate troops remained in the field, or possibly to the trans-Mississippi; but his cabinet members were more concerned with getting him safely out of the country. On May 10, 1865, Federal horsemen captured Jefferson Davis near Irwinville, Georgia, about fifty miles from the Florida state line. After a few days he was incarcerated at Fort Monroe, Virginia, where he spent the next two years.

By that time, Johnston had capitulated to Sherman and General Richard Taylor had surrendered most of the remaining Confederate troops east of the Mississippi. On May 26, the last Southern troops laid down their arms when General Edmund Kirby Smith, commanding the trans-Mississippi theater, surrendered his department. The Civil War was over.

The Legacy of the War

In terms of its impact on the United States, the Civil War remains the pivotal episode in American history. Like the near-contemporaneous wars of Italian and German unification, the American conflict took a fairly loose gathering of states and welded them into a nation. Politically it destroyed the concept of extreme states' rights and established the principle that the Union was perpetual. Its impact on American society was no less great. Not only did it result in the emancipation of 3.5 million African-Americans, it also ensured that thenceforward the mainstream of American civilization would be the industrial North, not the agrarian South.

Its significance in the history of warfare was no less great. Even more than the campaigns at the end of the Napoleonic Wars, the Civil War displayed the ascendancy of the defense over the offense, the inability of armies to destroy one another in battle, and the corresponding need to think in terms of a strategy of exhaustion or attrition rather than annihilation. The increased size of armies accounted for part of their enhanced resiliency; so too did the use of the corps, which enabled separate army wings to fight effectively on their own until reinforcements could come to their assistance. Only when Civil War armies allowed themselves to be surrounded and besieged (as at Vicksburg), or when they had previously exhausted themselves through prolonged offensives (as at Nashville) did it prove possible to destroy them.

A second important feature of the conflict was such sociopolitical factors as mass armies, conscription, and the mobilization of entire societies for war. The wars of the French Revolution and Napoleon had also witnessed these developments, but the Civil War carried them to a higher pitch, perhaps because both the Union and the Confederacy were among the most political societies then on earth. Both Northern and Southern soldiers were motivated in no small measure by strongly held beliefs about the causes for which they were fighting. The Western world had seen something like this during the wars of the American and French revolutions and, more recently, the struggles for Greek and Italian liberation. Otherwise one would have to reach back into the sixteenth- and seventeenth-century wars of religion for a parallel.

Third, the Civil War also saw the harnessing of the Industrial Revolution to the emergent forces of popular sovereignty and nationalism. New technologies played an enormous role in the conflict: railroads, rifles, and the telegraph, not to mention such naval innovations as turret-firing guns, iron-clad warships, and so on. Both the Union and the Confederacy worked diligently to exploit their industrial resources to the fullest; the North in particular evolved effective ways to organize and distribute their industrial output to armies in the field. The U.S. Military Railroads under Brigadier General Daniel C. McCallum, for example, achieved a record of energy and efficiency that any European army would have envied.

The Civil War also witnessed the great marches of destruction undertaken by Union forces during the war's final years and highly reminiscent of the English during the Hundred Years' War, numerous armies during the Thirty Years' War, and the French in 1688–1689. Often mistaken for an anticipation of twentieth-century strategic bombing, the Union raids against Southern war resources had much stronger continuities with past experience. The chief difference was that whereas the soldiers of the *ancien régime* in Europe had inflicted much indiscriminate mayhem, the greater political and moral awareness of the Civil War soldier—still thoroughly rooted in the ethical norms of his community—meant that Union armies conducted their attacks on Southern war resources with much greater discrimination. Depredations occurred, but wholesale killing of Southern civilians certainly did not. Private homes were rarely destroyed except in retaliation for guerrilla activity, and rapes—at least of white women—were uncommon. A much larger number of African-American women were assaulted and sexually abused. Taken together, the extensive mobilization of Northern and Southern societies, coupled with the large-scale union attacks on Southern crops and war resources, marked the first appearance of the total war dynamic that would become a pronounced characteristic of many twentieth-century struggles.

Finally, a word is in order about the strategic and operational conduct of the war. In general its quality, on both sides, was quite high. Both governments responded intelligently to the nature of the conflict and adopted realistic strategies. Of the two commanders-in-chief, Lincoln was clearly more able than Jefferson Davis, but then Lincoln was probably one of the three or four greatest statesmen of the past two centuries. Union and Confederate generalship was about equal. If the South had Lee and Jackson, it also had Bragg and Pemberton. Similarly, such lackluster Northern commanders as McClellan and Burnside were more than offset by Grant, Sherman, and Sheridan. Both sides fought according to the Napoleonic model, but both learned to adapt to the rather different logistical conditions of warfare in the vast, largely rural South. Each side eventually grasped the greatly changed tactical environment created by the rifled musket, and each made extensive use of field fortifications. This sound defensive solution, however, was not matched by an equivalent solution on the offensive. Both armies, despite scattered experiments with more open formations and tactics, continued to rely heavily on the traditional, practically shoulder-to-shoulder battle line.

Ultimately, however, the harsh realities of the Civil War battlefield did give a major impetus to the increasing professionalism of officers. It was obvious that largely untrained citizen-officers could not adequately cope with the demands of mid-nineteenth-century warfare, nor could regular officers whose imaginations were geared to skirmishing with Native American war parties. Deeply impressed by the failures of Civil War officership and the attendant waste of manpower, military reformers like Lieutenant Colonel Emory Upton waged a passionate crusade in favor of better professional education and standards. Upton's peers and disciples studied European armies, lobbied for advanced military schools and war colleges, and attempted to drag the United States Army thoroughly into the modern industrialized age. Although it required decades to complete, the result was a new cycle of military reform that prepared American armed forces, albeit imperfectly, to meet the challenges of a violent new century.

SUGGESTED READINGS

Barrett, John G. *Sherman's March Through the Carolinas* (Chapel Hill: University of North Carolina Press, 1956).

Beringer, Richard E., et al. *Why the South Lost the Civil War* (Athens: University of Georgia Press, 1986).

Castel, Albert. *Decision in the West: The Atlanta Campaign, 1864* (Lawrence: University Press of Kansas, 1992).

Catton, Bruce. *Grant Takes Command* (Boston: Little, Brown, 1969).

———. *A Stillness at Appomattox* (New York: Doubleday, 1952).

Donald, David H., ed. *Why the North Won the Civil War* (Baton Rouge: Louisiana State University Press, 1962).

Fowler, William M. *Under Two Flags: The American Navy in the Civil War* (New York: Norton, 1990).

Glatthaar, Joseph T. *The March to the Sea and Beyond: Sherman's Troops in the Savannah and Carolinas Campaigns* (New York: New York University Press, 1985).

Horn, Stanley F. *The Decisive Battle of Nashville* (Baton Rouge: Louisiana State University Press, 1956).

Marszalek, John F. *Sherman: A Soldier's Passion for Order* (New York: Free Press, 1992).

Matter, William D. *"If It Takes All Summer": The Battle of Spotsylvania* (Chapel Hill: University of North Carolina Press, 1988).

Reed, Rowena. *Combined Operations in the Civil War* (Annapolis: Naval Institute Press, 1978).

Rhea, Gordon C. *The Battle of the Wilderness, May 5–6, 1864* (Chapel Hill: University of North Carolina Press, 1994).

Still, William N., Jr. *Iron Afloat: The Story of the Confederate Armorclads* (Baton Rouge: Louisiana State University Press, 1970).

Sword, Wiley. *Embrace An Angry Wind: The Confederacy's Last Hurrah: Spring Hill, Franklin, and Nashville* (New York: HarperCollins, 1992).

Trudeau, Noah Andre. *Bloody Roads South: The Wilderness to Cold Harbor, May–June, 1864* (Boston: Little, Brown, 1989).

———. *The Last Citadel: Petersburg, Virginia, June 1864–April 1865* (Boston: Little, Brown, 1991).

———. *Out of the Storm: The End of the Civil War, April–June 1865* (Boston: Little, Brown, 1994).

Wert, Jeffry D. *From Winchester to Cedar Creek: The Shenandoah Campaign of 1864* (Carlisle, Penn.: South Mountain Press, 1987).

Wise, Steven A. *Lifeline of the Confederacy: The Blockade Runners* (Columbia: University of South Carolina Press, 1987).

PHOTOGRAPH CREDITS

Chapter 1: p. 5, New York Historical Society; p. 8, Indiana Historical Society; p. 10, Courtesy of the Historic New Orleans Collection, Museum Research Center, Acc. No. 1958.98.6; p. 12, Anne S. K. Brown Military Collection, Brown University Library; p. 15, Library of Congress; p. 17, Library of Congress; p. 19, Library of Congress; p. 25, Beverly R. Robinson Collection, U.S. Naval Academy Museum; p. 27, Courtesy of the West Point Museum, United States Military Academy, West Point, NY. **Chapter 2:** p. 37, Library of Congress; p. 39, Library of Congress; p. 41, National Archives; p. 50, Library of Congress; p. 53, Beverly R. Robinson Collection, U.S. Naval Academy Museum; p. 58, Library of Congress. **Chapter 3:** p. 63, Library of Congress; p. 68, Valentine Museum; p. 72, Library of Congress; p. 75, Library of Congress; p. 76, Library of Congress; p. 81, American Heritage Picture Collection; p. 82, M. and M. Karolik Collection, Museum of Fine Arts; p. 84, Print Collection. Miriam and Ira D. Wallach Division of Art, Prints and Photographs. The New York Public Library. Astor, Lenox and Tilden Foundations. **Chapter 4:** p. 99, Valentine Museum; p. 101, National Archives; p. 103, Library of Congress; p. 110, U.S. Naval Historical Center; p. 111, Library of Congress; p. 117, Library of Congress; p. 118, National Archives; p. 125, William Gladstone Collection. **Chapter 5:** p. 131, National Archives; p. 134, Library of Congress; p. 143, Library of Congress; p. 144, National Archives; p. 150, National Gallery of Art, Washington, D.C. gift of Edgar William and Bernice Chrysler Garbisch; p. 152, Courtesy, Peabody & Essex Museum, Salem, MA; p. 156, Copyright by White House Historical Association; Photograph by National Geographic Society.

Index